AF614837

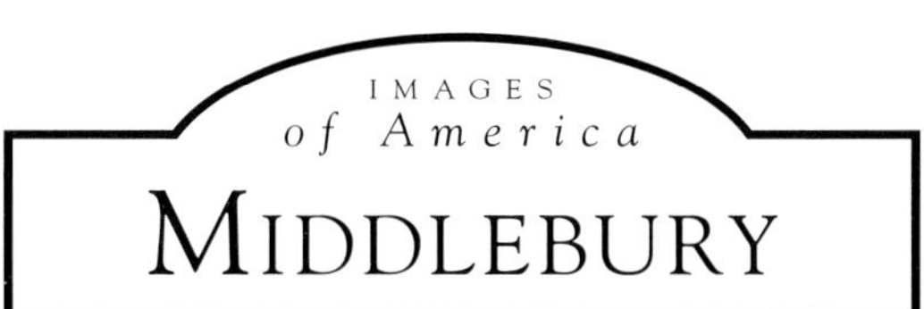
IMAGES
of America
MIDDLEBURY

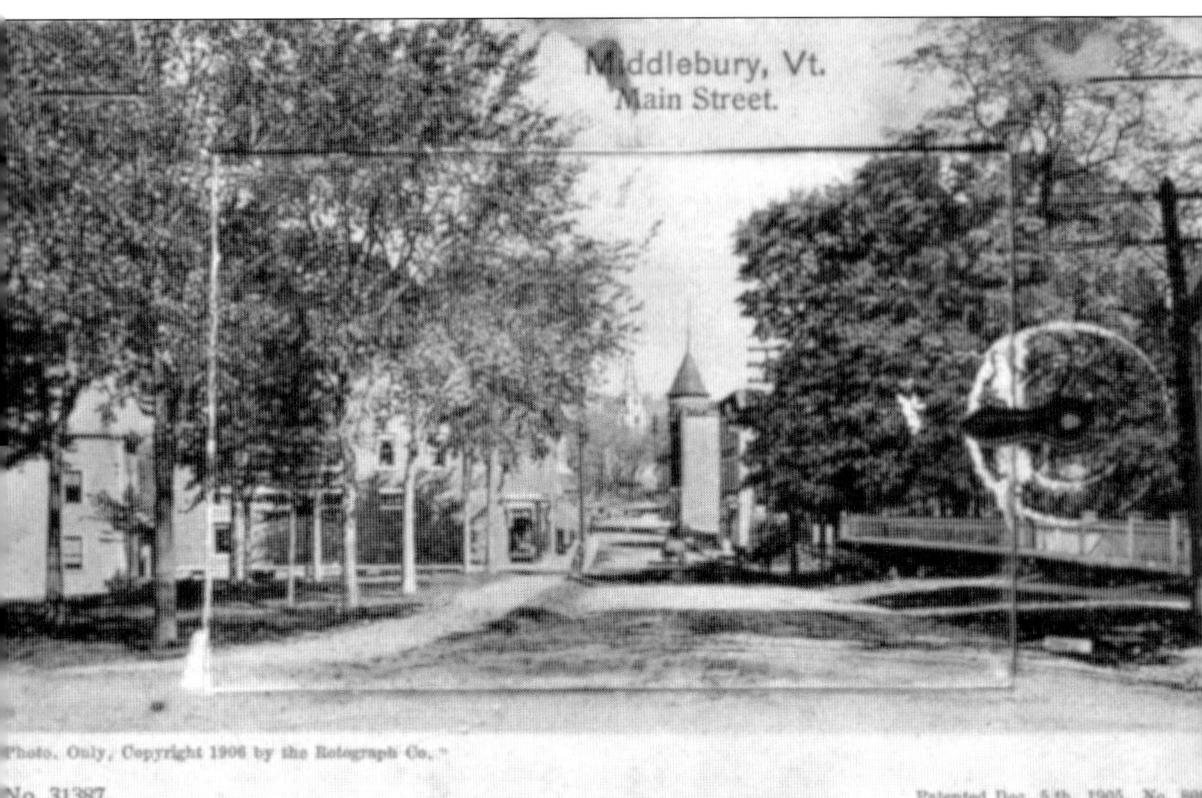

The town of Middlebury has long been the subject of many photographs and picture postcards. This one has been creatively altered by the sender. A little door with a revolving latch has been cut into the cover of the card. There are 12 small scenes folded under the door: the town hall, Main Street showing the Episcopal and Congregational churches, the courthouse, the Baptist church, Starr Library, Old Chapel, Warner Science Hall, St. Mary's Church and rectory, the College Street Graded School, the Civil War monument, the railroad trestle bridge, and the falls of Otter Creek. Beneath the cover of this book, a history of the town of Middlebury also lies hidden, as well as more than one love story. (Courtesy of Middlebury College Special Collections.)

ON THE COVER: Prior to the automobile's swift rise to dominance, persons of means had a special relationship with their family's grooms and drivers. For those who could afford them, they were more than merely hired help. When Henry Sheldon was picked for the honor of having his carriage be the first one across the new stone bridge in 1893, he accepted, and it was official. On arrival, he announced himself to be the first man across. His driver, Marshall Butterfield, corrected him: "Not quite," he said dryly, in true laconic Vermont style. (Courtesy of the Henry Sheldon Museum Stewart-Swift Research Center.)

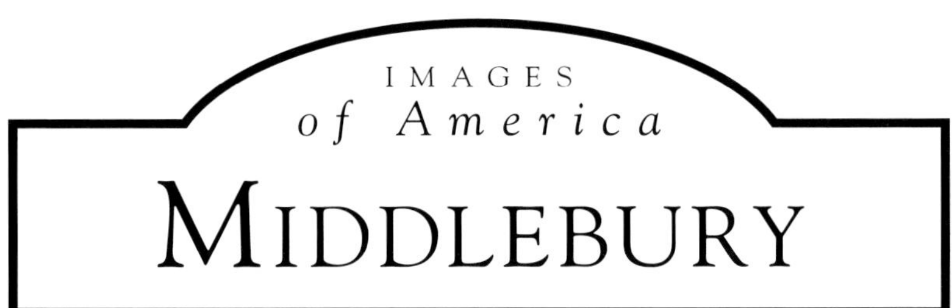

David Munford

ISBN 978-1-4671-0517-0

Published by Arcadia Publishing
Charleston, South Carolina

Printed in the United States of America

Library of Congress Control Number: 2019957668

For all general information, please contact Arcadia Publishing:
Telephone 843-853-2070
Fax 843-853-0044
E-mail sales@arcadiapublishing.com
For customer service and orders:
Toll-Free 1-888-313-2665

Visit us on the Internet at www.arcadiapublishing.com

This book is dedicated to my parents, Howard and Marion Munford, who met and were married at Middlebury College. For many years, they were enthusiastically involved with both college and town, and their home was generously open to all.

Contents

Acknowledgments

This project would have foundered at every stage without my wife, Tami, who tirelessly supplied me with editing skills and insights, technological expertise, moral support, and general encouragement. The majority of the images were made available by Eva Garcelon-Hart and the staff of the Henry Sheldon Museum. I give my heartfelt appreciation to Danielle Rougeau of Middlebury College Special Collections. At the Ilsley Library, Judy Holler proved herself a dogged researcher, and library director Dana Hart provided my connection with Arcadia Publishing. My thanks to the National Bank for allowing the use of Colonel Ilsley's portrait. Glenn Andres's *A Walking History of Middlebury* was an invaluable source of information. My editor Caroline Anderson is a patient angel. Finally, I owe much to my late mentors Arthur Healy and Storrs Lee, who set me on my professional path long before I could see it for myself.

All images used in this book are courtesy of the Henry Sheldon Museum Stewart-Swift Research Center unless otherwise noted.

Introduction

Middlebury's geography is the product of the Laurentide Ice Sheet. When the glacier retreated, the area saw its first human visitors. These were nomadic hunters using boats made from animal hide to navigate the brackish arm of the North Atlantic that stretched five hundred miles south from the Gulf of St. Lawrence.

Much later came the recorded history of hardy pioneers, Mohawk raiding parties, Redcoats, Tory loyalists, German mercenaries, visionary educators, 28 men lost in the Civil War, and the mild rivalry between two philanthropists that changed the face of the town. The early 19th century even featured a slave-owning embezzler who cleaned out the bank vault and escaped across the border into Canada. Every epic story needs its villain.

Middlebury owes its existence to its falls. Otter Creek provided not only an avenue of transportation through the wilderness, but at this spot, its falls also offered a source of waterpower. Before the Revolutionary War, canny settlers had spotted the territory's potential. Above the falls was a ford. Nearby were the first sawmill, a blockhouse, and a rudimentary schoolhouse. When Maj. Christopher Carleton's British raiders and their allies burned the small village in 1778, most of its inhabitants had fled south to safety. A notable exception to this was the resolute widow Ann Story, who defiantly stayed with her family about a mile south from where the raiders stopped and turned around. When everyone else returned to rebuild during peacetime, they knew exactly what they needed to do.

Middlebury takes its name from its location at the midpoint between Salisbury and New Haven, both towns whose names reflect their founders' origins in Connecticut. One of the leaders of the group from Connecticut was Gamaliel Painter, a man of immense practicality and vision who had spent the war years as George Washington's chief of engineers. He had the professional's sharp eye for terrain and quickly bought up the new town's high ground, parceling out plots of land as patronage.

Middlebury straddles a band of Vermont marble, and from early on, this resource caused an industry to spring up in Frog Hollow below the falls as well as at Belden and Halpin Falls on the northern and eastern edges of town. As the 19th century began, other opportunities presented themselves, and Painter's group acted swiftly. Their connection to Yale University facilitated the founding of Middlebury College in 1800. Soon afterward, Gamaliel Painter's shrewd political skills awarded the town new civic status as the official county seat.

Around this time, another visionary arrived from Connecticut. Emma Hart was a young woman with enlightened ideas and a clear sense of mission. Her determination was focused on education for females, and she would not be deterred. By the time she and her husband, John Willard, left Middlebury to establish the Emma Willard School in Troy, New York, she had left a permanent mark on American education.

In 1823, Middlebury College graduated its first African American freeman, Alexander Twilight, who went on to a long and distinguished career. Frederick Douglas came to town in 1836 at the invitation of an abolitionist lawyer. The Underground Railroad had a stop downtown, with an escape route to Otter Creek. Middlebury was involved in the great issues of the day, and when the Rutland Railroad arrived, the town took advantage of this new improvement in transportation for both freight and passenger service. Rail service also provided a new connection between the town and the outside world.

When Abraham Lincoln issued his call for volunteers in 1861, both town and college responded. Veterans returned to a growing and prosperous Middlebury, a trend that, during the Victorian Era, would see the construction of more of the town's distinctive architecture. The face of downtown was ravaged by fire in 1891, and 11 structures were demolished. In reaction to this calamity, one of Middlebury's main benefactors, Joseph Battell, installed a modern system of firefighting and provided funding for a stone bridge to replace the damaged wooden one. In addition, he had a major block of stores and apartments designed, bearing his name. Battered by the flood of 1927, the Battell Bridge stood firm. Battell himself also refused to budge in his implacable opposition to the internal combustion engine, and as owner of *The Middlebury Register*, used his newspaper as a means to highlight each and every automobile accident he could find out about.

Another important town personage at the time was Col. Silas Ilsley, a Civil War veteran who had made his fortune in tin. He and his wife occupied a suite in the Middlebury Inn. As laconic as Joseph Battell was loquacious, Colonel Ilsley donated funding for the Civil War Monument, the Memorial Baptist Church, and the Ilsley Library. He also provided the town with the Addison County Fairgrounds, which boasted the largest grandstand in the state. When Colonel Ilsley died, he bequeathed a generous amount to Middlebury College as well as to his favorite groom.

Despite the arrival of the automobile, Middlebury was proud of its association with the Morgan horse. Horses and oxen were used as draft animals well into the 20th century, and as late as 1948, a sign on the edge of the town green proclaimed a spot reserved for horses only.

As it had in the Civil War, Middlebury sent volunteers to fight in both World War I and World War II. When the Greatest Generation returned, they had had enough excitement. They wanted a peaceful community in which to raise their families, and Middlebury found its ongoing identity as a comfortably balanced community of "town and gown." The college enrollment was boosted by the GI Bill and expanded as a result, doubling and tripling in size.

In 1996, the Frank Mahady Courthouse became Middlebury's third and most modern one. As Middlebury's streets were still those of a horse and buggy town, traffic congestion had become an issue that clearly had to be dealt with. The year 2010 saw the completion of the Cross Street Bridge, featuring the longest pre-cast span in the United States. In 2016, the new town hall received the Greenest Building Award.

The history of Middlebury, Vermont, is thoroughly documented, and since it has always proven to be popular with photographers and artists, it is also well-illustrated.

One

Early Visitors, Founders, and Visionaries

On its way to Lake Champlain, Otter Creek divides Middlebury east to west, but cannot avoid a north and south split as well. This separation caused both social and political rivalries in the town's early history. By the time this map was drawn, there had been some changes. The original survey, for example, indicated that land just south of the town center belonged to Weybridge. Resurveyed, it became Cornwall, until Gamaliel Painter's legal team successfully petitioned the legislature to appropriate it for Middlebury. This maneuver was particularly fortuitous for Seth Storrs, who had been quietly buying up abutting parcels on the high ground looking west toward the Adirondacks. (Courtesy of Middlebury College Special Collections.)

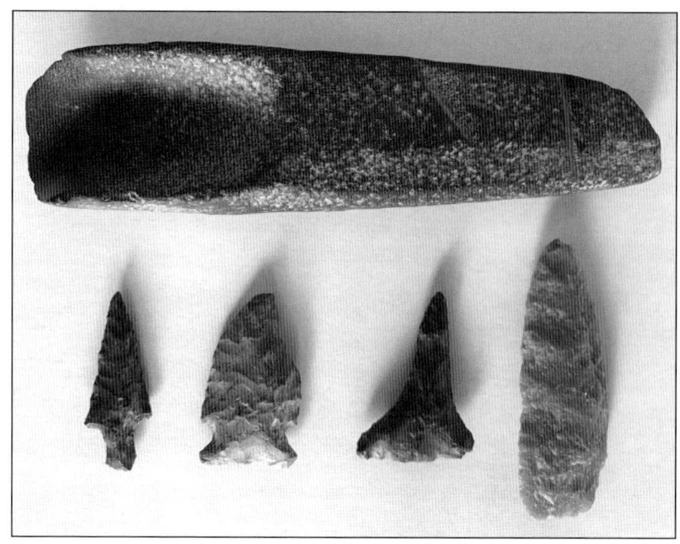

Otter Creek is also called the "Indian Road." Long before Middlebury was a settlement, aboriginal peoples traveled through the area. They were adept at creating the tools and weapons they needed from materials at hand. Examples are seen in this gouge, drill, knife, and arrowheads found in Middlebury, all over a thousand years old. The Abenakis of the late Woodland period native to the Middlebury area were uprooted and disrupted by the arrival of Europeans. (Author's collection.)

Middlebury was chartered in 1761 by Gov. Benning Wentworth. The name came from its middle location between the towns of New Haven and Salisbury. Many of the earliest residents of European origin were farmers. Their chief crops were hay and grains. The glacial kame in the northern part of Middlebury was originally named Mt. Nebo after the biblical location where Moses died, but was renamed Chipman Hill after the resolute Chipman family. This c. 1860 photograph shows the rural nature of Seminary Street with a cow in the foreground and a half-cleared Chipman Hill pasture in the background. In 1860, Middlebury's population was 2,879. At the 2010 census, the population was 8,496.

During the 18th century, Connecticut had become home to a restless group of individuals eyeing the beckoning wilderness to their north. John Chipman and Gamaliel Painter uprooted themselves in 1773 and struggled north toward a new life. Painter saw his future in the power of the falls on Otter Creek. He secured that location but was delayed by the Revolutionary War, in which he distinguished himself as George Washington's artificer. After he returned to pursue his dream, Middlebury had sprouted as many taverns as mills. Gamaliel Painter became sheriff. Stocks and a whipping post were prominently located on the town green. There is no evidence of either being used. When Painter became judge, his plea-bargained sentences often involved pulling stumps from the green. Painter outlived his first wife and all his children. His daughter Abby had been his favorite, and her death was a deeply felt tragedy. As a stoic Vermont Yankee, Painter buried himself in work, serving both town and gown with all his available energy until his death at age 76. (Courtesy of Middlebury College Special Collections.)

When Gamaliel Painter became judge, envisioning Middlebury as the future county seat, he needed a suitably impressive residence where the patriarch could overlook his fiefdom from his hilltop. In 1802, work was completed on a mansion built partly by a new and talented young joiner, Lavius Fillmore. The house remains a showpiece of Federal-style detail and majestic presence. Painter had balanced God-fearing humility with well-earned pride. Every year, Middlebury residents entered through the Ionic columns to attend a lavish Christmas party here, relieving them briefly from the loneliness of frontier life.

In the competition between the "north-enders" and the "south-enders," the Foote clan took a blow in 1787 when they lost their mill foreman, Simeon Dudley. Gamaliel Painter paid Dudley to switch sides and build the town's first frame house on the ridge overlooking Painter's mills. When it was done, Painter moved in with his family, adding a second story. When Painter's new grand residence was built next door, the humble Dudley house was moved downhill to Seymour Street.

Addison County was founded in 1785 but lacked a county seat. Gamaliel Painter's connection with the state legislature resulted in Middlebury becoming a shire town in 1790. The first Addison County Courthouse was constructed in 1796 on one of Painter's building lots. The structure was notoriously hard to heat. When the legislature met there, they chose to adjourn to a tavern. The belfry was later struck by lightning and never replaced. Finally, the building was transported to the entrance of the Addison County Fairgrounds, and its name was changed from Exhibition Hall to Floral Hall. It was dismantled in 1939.

In 1819, Daniel Adams published his *Geography, Or, A Description Of The World: In Three Parts*. On page 111, he wrote, "Middlebury, on that same river [Otter Creek], 20 miles from the lake, in which is a college, a courthouse, a gaol, a brewery, a gun and card factory, a forge, printing office, and a number of sawmills." Whether spelled "gaol' or "jail," every town of a sufficient size needed one. This thick-walled stone structure was built by Jabez Rogers in 1811. During the 1840s, it was purchased by Oliver Washington, who had it converted to a private residence.

Horatio Seymour was a man of substance and wisdom. He was a lawyer and postmaster of Middlebury from 1800 to 1809. Seymour was elected to the US Senate in 1821. He had enough vision to endorse the creation of the female seminary, opening the way for Emma Hart Willard. During the construction of Seymour's lavish home in 1816–1817, its owner confessed concerns about its considerable expense. The results proved his gamble worthwhile. Located at 3 Main Street, it is now the town community house.

In 1807, the director of the Middlebury Female Seminary became ill. The search for a replacement led to a seismic shift in American education. Her successor was Emma Hart, an enlightened young woman driven by a strong sense of mission. After moving to Middlebury from Connecticut, Hart plunged into her new job as teacher and administrator. Her favorite subject was geometry. Two years later, she married Dr. John Willard, a widower and a pillar of the community. In 1818, Emma showed her handwritten opus, *A Plan for Improving Female Education*, to the governor of New York, who shared it with his legislature. Her efforts eventually ensured women's right to coeducation. This monument to Emma Willard was dedicated in 1941. It stands on the green triangle in front of the Congregational church.

By 1800, Addison County had developed a reputation as a magnet for bold, fearless men. These were men who had earned their rights the hard way and liked to point that out, loudly and often. They would consent to the rule of law but never to arbitrary decisions. Yale-educated lawyer and college founder Seth Storrs was one of these men. Although his portrait portrays him as a rather dour fellow, he must have also had a softer side, as the inscription on his headstone in Middlebury's West Cemetery implies: "Seth Storrs and Electra Stone / Were married Nov. 26, 1789, / and removed to Middlebury in 1794. / For nearly half a century, they were united on earth. / Are they not now together for a blissful eternity?" (Courtesy of Middlebury College Special Collections.)

This is the home Seth Storrs and his son-in-law built on South Street. The gray limestone pathway leads to one granite step followed by five of white marble. The house faces northwest, and the porch is monumental Greek revival. The façade provides clear evidence that white marble's dramatic contrast with brick has provided Middlebury's builders with inspiration from early in the town's history.

At the dawn of the 19th century, Middlebury could boast a college charter, several academies, a grammar school, a courthouse, various mills, and a number of taverns. What was conspicuously absent was any house of worship. Lavius Fillmore, a young architect from Connecticut, was offered the chance to fill this vacuum for a legal share in the crucial water rights driving prosperous local industry. In a symbolic gesture, the former site of a tavern was chosen for the location, and work was begun on the Congregational church. Businessmen were expected to purchase a family pew in advance. The church was completed in 1809. (Courtesy of Middlebury College Special Collections.)

Constructed from the same gray stone used to build both the mills and the college, Middlebury had its second church in 1826. The town's convenient fusion of worship and finance lasted until a group of Middlebury's founding fathers took advantage of Vermont's recent statehood status to invoke freedom of religion. The origins of St. Stephen's Episcopal Church were attributable to the auspices of the Episcopal Society, founded in 1805. Early members included Horatio Seymour and, ironically, Fillmore. This loophole provided a means to circumvent the Congregationalist monopoly. The bell tower's crenellations are suggestive of battlements. When they were restored in the 1970s, Arthur Healy wondered if the Episcopalians intended to open fire on the Congregationalists.

The Order of Freemasonry is venerable (the Mother Grand Lodge was formed in 1717) and has included many luminaries. It has been exemplified by symbols and rituals, and early in the 19th century became the target of conspiracy theory to the point of having to go underground. By the time Middlebury's Masonic Hall was constructed on Court Square in 1823, Freemasons had become rehabilitated. Later, the Addison County Courthouse was built next door on the right.

Just to the south of the hill bearing his family name, Yale-educated lawyer Daniel Chipman built his three-story law school in 1816. In 1827, the property was purchased by the Female School Association, which then modified the structure to house the female seminary. Seminary Street was named after this institution, which then underwent a number of additions and remodelings until around 1910, when it was razed and 42 Seminary Street became the site of the new Congregational parsonage. (Courtesy of Middlebury College Special Collections.)

Two

Schools and Middlebury College

After Middlebury's first schoolhouse was burned in Carleton's Raid, the town's children were instructed as best they could by meeting in scattered private homes. Gamaliel Painter, Seth Storrs, Daniel Chipman, and their cohorts were not satisfied with this arrangement, so Painter used his political muscle to have the legislature charter the Addison County Grammar School, one of the oldest corporations in Vermont. Storrs made the largest contribution with $350, an immense sum at the time. In 1798, the result, built on the west side of town, was the 40-by-80-foot, three-story wooden academy building, "free and forever exempt from taxes." Boys attending the school had to be at least nine years old and prepared to go to worship every Sunday. Tuition was $3 a quarter for "common English studies" and $4 for "those who are preparing for College."

In contrast to the academy, the Case Street School was a traditional one-room building, designed by Middlebury's Clinton Smith. Often, one-room schoolhouses presented the challenge of multi-aged grouping, but many noted public figures owed their education to this system.

In the spirit of modernizing education, the academy building was replaced by the brick College Street School, also featuring three stories and a more ornate cupola. The school burned in 1904 but was soon rebuilt, retaining its brownstone detailing and a gable facing each cardinal direction. The cupola was not replaced. More recently, the interior was extensively remodeled, and the building is now named Twilight Hall after Middlebury College's first African American graduate.

Included in the College Street School were classrooms, a library, a laboratory, dormitories, and a chapel. When Middlebury College was founded in 1800, it shared the building with the grammar school until 1805. Note the public well on the corner of South Main and College Streets in the foreground around 1870.

As the oldest college building in Vermont, Painter Hall is also a monument to Vermont practicality and civic pride. Both masons and materials were locally available. Experienced mill builders knew what to do. Completed in 1816, the result was both handsome and versatile. Its eight chimneys served multiple fireplaces. Over time, Painter Hall has housed classrooms, a dormitory, a library, and a gymnasium. (Courtesy of Middlebury College Special Collections.)

Multipurpose architecture by way of basic mill design had proven a success. Now, the young college needed more classrooms, a library, and a chapel. On the next lot south from Painter Hall, foundations for the chapel were laid in 1835, and in 1836, the building was finished, including a number of added flourishes. The eastward-facing façade features a clock tower topped by a cupola and a weathervane. The double outside stairs are decorated with wrought-iron railings. The design was inspired by the Old Chapel on the venerable campus of Yale, mother institution to Middlebury College. (Courtesy of Middlebury College Special Collections.)

For balance and in hopes of potentially increasing enrollment, another version of Painter Hall was planned. Some funding was left over for building on the plot of land to the south of Old Chapel. The final years of the 1830s did not go smoothly for the college, and enrollments actually dropped. Finally, by 1860, Starr Hall was constructed, only to be gutted by fire in 1864. Donations enabled a rebuilding effort, and by 1885, reforms and improvements had brought the college back from its decline. Starr Hall was completed. (Courtesy of Middlebury College Special Collections.)

As the college anticipated its centennial celebration, Pres. Ezra Brainerd had to decide between a new science building and a library. The library won. The gift of Charles and Egbert Starr, the first marble building on campus was a classic temple of knowledge. It was completed in 1900, barely in time for the ceremony, with students throwing themselves into a last-minute effort to fill the shelves before the deadline. Using stretchers and wheelbarrows, they finished the job minutes before the arrival of the centennial crowd. By 1928, the original building had been outgrown, especially after the donation of the Julian Abernathy collection of American literature, and the building was considerably expanded. (Courtesy of Middlebury College Special Collections.)

The interior of Starr Library, complete with fireplace and arched coffered ceiling, shows how magnificent the Abernathy Reading Room was. Indeed, it has been considered by many to be the most beautiful room in Vermont. (Author's collection.)

The Vermont Constitution guaranteed no Vermont resident of African ancestry need fear becoming enslaved; racial prejudice and indentured servitude, however, remained. Alexander Twilight purchased his freedom at age 20, and in 1823 received his degree from Middlebury College, thus becoming the first African American citizen to graduate from a college or university. He went on to become a minister, a member of the Vermont General Assembly, and an educator. He met Mercy Merrill in upstate New York, married her in 1826, and returned to Vermont. He designed, paid for, and hand-built a four-story granite schoolhouse in Brownington, Vermont. Athenian Hall became the hub of Brownington Academy, where he presided over his creation as teacher and administrator, never neglecting his calling as a minister. Alexander Twilight was the type of individual who believed in leading by example, and he proved it by living his beliefs. (Courtesy of Orleans County Historical Society and the Brownington Museum.)

In 1867, a house was built to reflect the Italianate style of the College Street School directly opposite. It was also the residence of the fifth Middlebury College president, Harvey Kitchel. In 1891, it was renamed Battell Hall and served as the first female dormitory for the college. It may have been the result of a meeting of trustees in 1883, when the president at the time, Cyrus Hamlin, was a little hard of hearing and approved "the same privileges to young ladies as young gentlemen." Once this appeared in writing, there was no taking it back. Mary Belle Chellis, valedictorian in 1886, set an example for the young women who were later to reside in this handsome house. (Courtesy of Middlebury College Special Collections.)

Always ready for a joke, Jackson photography studio produced this gentle Victorian comment on the gender-segregated campus, as well as indulging in the running gag of having men dressed, in this case, in women's nightgowns. (Courtesy of Middlebury College Special Collections.)

This student is taking advantage of a quiet moment to study in her dormitory room, probably in the original Battell Hall, around 1900. She has decorated her walls extensively with photographs and a Middlebury College pennant. On her bureau is a wind-up alarm clock. (Courtesy of Middlebury College Special Collections.)

In 1915, college students needed a way to have their luggage carried from the railroad depot to campus and vice versa. The Middlebury College commissioner of transportation and his faithful horse were up to the job.

Students entered the Middlebury College campus via a long path lined with towering elms. The path led from the College Street Schoolhouse, later named Twilight Hall, up to Starr Library and Old Stone Row.

This view of the college's Old Stone Row from the cupola of the College Street School became permanently unavailable in 1904, when fire gutted the school, and the vantage point was not replaced. The buildings are, from left to right, Starr Hall, Old Chapel, and Painter Hall. (Courtesy of Middlebury College Special Collections.)

John Griffith McCullough moved to Vermont in 1873 and served as the president of the Bennington & Rutland Railroad as well as a term as governor. His donation was the base for the funding allowing the McCollough Gymnasium to be constructed in 1912. As with other college architecture, the style was Georgian, and the building material was local marble. It was used by male students until 1949, when it was opened to coeducation. (Courtesy of Middlebury College Special Collections.)

The confident-looking young men of this 1893 Middlebury College baseball team are facing the impending turn of the century with optimism. The world order, in general, was stable. (Courtesy of Middlebury College Special Collections.)

Catherine Emma Robbins (left) graduated from Middlebury in 1923. She and friends Hilda Kurth (center) and Kathleen Norris (right) created their own hiking club in 1927, "the Three Musketeers." The young women took on the Long Trail end to end, living up to their motto: "The Musketeers must get there!" They are pictured above taking a break after reaching Hazen's Notch. The annotated *Long Trail Guidebook* below was provided by Catherine Robbins's granddaughter Cara Nelson, who retraced the Musketeers' hike 70 years later with another Musketeer granddaughter, Amity Robichaud. (Both, courtesy of Middlebury College Special Collections.)

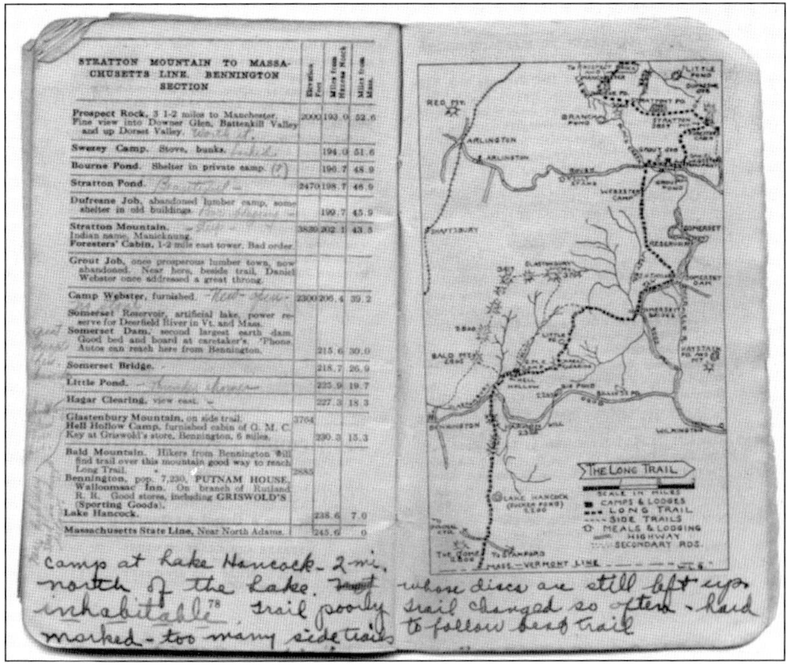

STRATTON MOUNTAIN TO MASSACHUSETTS LINE. BENNINGTON SECTION	Elevation Feet	Miles from [illegible]	Miles from Mass.
Prospect Rock. 3 1-2 miles to Manchester. Fine view into Downer Glen, Battenkill Valley and up Dorset Valley.	2000	192.0	52.6
Sweezy Camp. Stove, bunks.		194.0	51.6
Bourne Pond. Shelter in private camp. (?)		196.7	48.9
Stratton Pond.	2470	198.7	46.9
Dufresne Job, abandoned lumber camp, some shelter in old buildings.		199.7	45.9
Stratton Mountain. Indian name, Manicknung. **Foresters' Cabin,** 1-2 mile east tower. Bad order.	3859	202.1	43.5
Grout Job, once prosperous lumber town, now abandoned. Near here, beside trail, Daniel Webster once addressed a great throng.			
Camp Webster, furnished.	2300	206.4	39.2
Somerset Reservoir, artificial lake, power reserve for Deerfield River in Vt. and Mass. **Somerset Dam,** second largest earth dam. Good bed and board at caretaker's. 'Phone. Autos can reach here from Bennington.		215.6	30.0
Somerset Bridge.		218.7	26.9
Little Pond.		225.9	19.7
Hagar Clearing, view east.		227.3	18.3
Glastenbury Mountain, on side trail. **Hell Hollow Camp,** furnished cabin of G. M. C. Key at Griswold's store, Bennington, 6 miles.	3764	230.3	15.3
Bald Mountain. Hikers from Bennington will find trail over this mountain good way to reach Long Trail. **Bennington,** pop. 7,230, **PUTNAM HOUSE,** Walloomsac Inn. On branch of Rutland R. R. Good stores, including **GRISWOLD'S** (Sporting Goods). **Lake Hancock.**	2885	238.6	7.0
Massachusetts State Line, Near North Adams.		245.6	0

78

With the passage of the 19th Amendment, women were finally given the right to vote. It was clear that times had changed and, with them, outmoded ideas of what females were capable of. By 1920, women were firmly established on campus and were allowed to play sports. Decorum of dress remained an issue, but Amelia Bloomer's invention proved practical for allowing freedom of movement. These letter-wearing members of the Middlebury women's basketball team exude confidence both on and off the court around 1920. (Courtesy of Middlebury College Special Collections.)

The steps of Old Chapel provided a popular and immediately recognizable location for group portraits. These students have included an older man who may have been on the faculty. The design of the bicycle dates the photograph to the 1890s.

These athletic stalwarts of 1924 represent both the tennis and the baseball teams, probably fraternity brothers, on the steps of Old Chapel. Only a few have chosen to wear uniforms, and perhaps for reasons of chivalry, a female classmate is included near the top of the stairs. (Courtesy of Middlebury College Special Collections.)

As part of the aftermath of World War II, the GI Bill brought a new wave of enrollment at the college. Existing facilities were strained, and there was no building on campus large enough for the entire student body to meet at once. A fundraising drive was dedicated to Middlebury men and women who had served in the war. Since McCullough Gymnasium was now cramped, a modern and expanded athletic center was needed. Memorial Field House, with its hockey rink, was completed in 1949. (Courtesy of Middlebury College Special Collections.)

Midway through the 19th century, waves of religious revivalism convulsed the student body on a regular basis, encouraged by presidents who regarded spiritual searching as an educational mission equal to the classics and rhetoric. Science was shoved into the background, but professors persevered, and in 1901, a new marble science building was almost ready. Funding dried up, leaving a shell, but further efforts to obtain funds prevailed. These provided the building with a red oak interior, sweeping balustrades, and glass-fronted display cases. Warner Science housed physics, biology, and chemistry departments and included a hemicycle auditorium. (Courtesy of Middlebury College Special Collections.)

Just to the west of Warner Science is this optimistic inscription on a marble memorial slab. It marks an endowment by a wealthy widower who tragically lost his wife in an airplane crash. (Courtesy of Middlebury College Special Collections.)

As with many buildings, both on campus and off, what was first constructed as a private residence was later, due to its location, taken over and transformed. In this case, merino sheep breeder Uriah D. Twitchell is seen with his family in front of his farmhouse on the crest of the hill with a dramatic view of the Adirondack Mountains. Mary Bolton (Peck) is on the right. The house was built in 1873. Later, it became Battell Cottage.

When Middlebury College admitted women in 1883, it was directly due to Joseph Battell that the facilities were made available to house them. In 1902, a separate campus for women was chartered. When college president Thomas asked Battell for help, the philanthropist obliged by buying up the property. This purchase included what was referred to as the Brainard Lane Farmhouse, which became part of the Northern Women's Campus. It is now the Adirondack House. (Courtesy of Middlebury College Special Collections.)

Middlebury graduate John A. Mead had been a doctor, a businessman, and a political figure, becoming governor of Vermont in 1910. The need for a new and bigger chapel had been evident for some time, and in 1916, on the 50th anniversary of his own graduation, Dr. Mead offered the funding. The entrance is classic Greek revival, as monumental as any temple. On the architrave are carved the words from Psalm 95:4: "The Strength of the Hills is His Also." Ascending skyward, the bell tower is done in Federal style. Initially, it housed 11 chimes, but some 70 years later, they were removed and replaced by a full carillon of 48 bells. Another impressive addition was the Gress-Miles pipe organ in the chancel. (Courtesy of Middlebury College Special Collections.)

For many years, attendance at chapel service was obligatory for students. Faculty members were also assigned their turn at delivering orations. Here, the service is over, and the student body is streaming down the hill to the dormitories. To the left is Hepburn Hall.

College trustee Alonzo Hepburn recognized that the "College on the Hill" is actually located on several of them, and he offered to build a dormitory structure to anchor the highest ridge, south of Mead Chapel. Hepburn Hall was the result, built in the Georgian style with a crowning cupola and panoramic views both east and west. The hall was built in 1916. (Courtesy of Middlebury College Special Collections.)

The lounge of the dormitory once displayed some trophy heads from Hepburn's hunting exploits and was thus nicknamed the "Hepburn Zoo." Hepburn made it clear that he did not want his building constructed from marble, as he had always associated that material with tombstones. For that reason, and perhaps influenced by the handsome downtown appearance of the Horatio Seymour house, Hepburn specified yellow brick. After his death, his gift was discreetly painted gray to match the stone buildings. (Courtesy of Middlebury College Special Collections.)

In 1927, Middlebury alumnus Charles Andrew Munroe was made a trustee after his career in law and business. In 1940, he perceived the need for a new building to house humanities and social sciences. The former college tennis courts provided a convenient location, and using the same Weybridge limestone as Old Stone Row, the Neo-Georgian result was Munroe Hall. From 1941, the entrance of Munroe Hall housed the "Winged Genie Pollinating the Date Palm" until it was removed for restoration in 1990. The alabaster relief from the 9th-century BCE Assyrian Empire was bequeathed to the college by alumnus Rev. Wilson A. Farnsworth in 1854. It is now on permanent display in the Middlebury College Museum of Art.

As an institution of liberal arts, Middlebury College has always been devoted to music and dance. This compact three-story brick building, erected in 1925 with its modest Greek revival porch, was the college music studio. It was torn down in 1958 to make way for Wright Memorial Theater. (Courtesy of Middlebury College Special Collections.)

CARR HALL-MIDDLEBURY COLLEGE

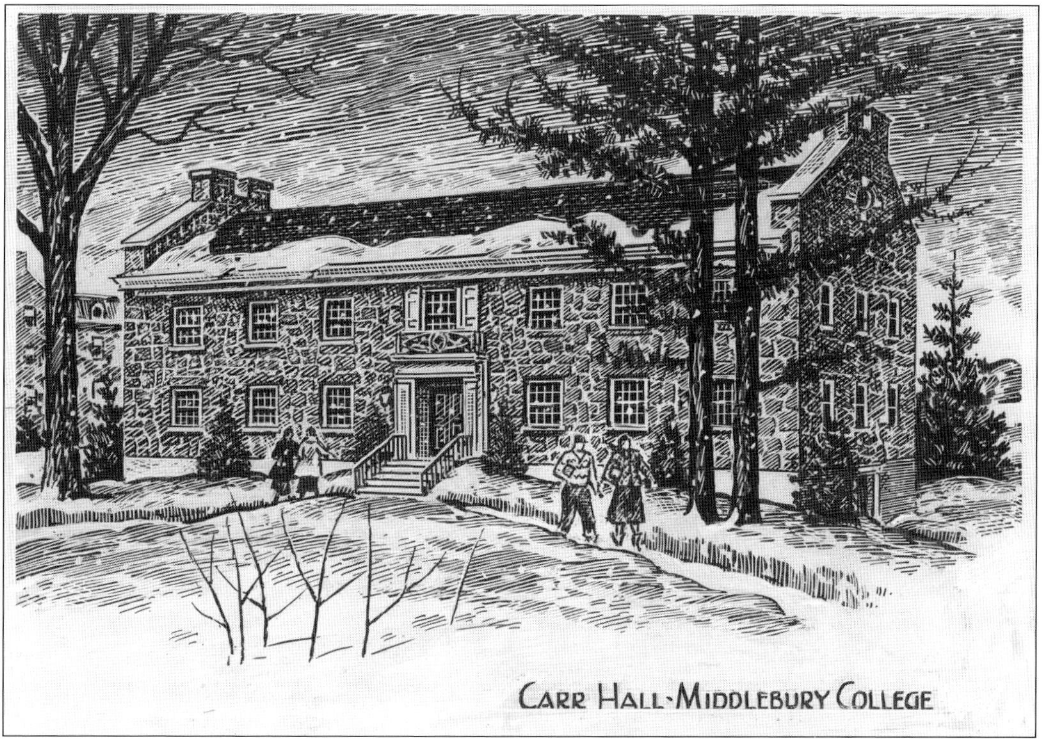

After graduating in 1901, Reid L. Carr, a native of Cornwall, went on to make a name for himself as a New York lawyer, businessman, and eventually, college trustee. In 1951, Carr Hall was constructed from local limestone to fit thematically with Munroe and Forest Halls. Upon Carr's retirement, the oak paneling from his New York office was transported to Middlebury to decorate the entrance lobby of Carr Hall. Until 1968, this building was home to the art department, with a fine arts library, classrooms, and studios. Then it served as an infirmary, with Campus Security in the basement. Scratchboard depictions such as this were very popular in the 1950s. (Courtesy of Middlebury College Special Collections.)

The town's philanthropists both remembered the college in their wills, and Joseph Battell, always generous with real estate, bequeathed over 30,000 acres in Ripton. Ten thousand of these were retained, creating a generous campus around the Breadloaf Inn. The rest, according to the will, could be sold, but only if the proceeds went toward developing the North Campus for women. The Ripton acreage was sold to the federal government as a national forest. The funds were used to construct Forest Hall, a Neo-Georgian building intended to be part of a larger but unrealized quadrangle. (Courtesy of Middlebury College Special Collections.)

In the spring of 1943, the college's graduating seniors had reason to be hopeful. Here, they are outside of Forest Hall, tapping their Gamaliel Painter canes together. Since 1819, the cane and its song have become an enduring symbol of courage at the college: "When Gamaliel Painter died, he was Middlebury's pride, a sturdy pioneer without a stain; and he left his all by will to the college on the hill, and included in the codicil his cane." All new alumni receive a replica of the cane. (Courtesy of Middlebury College Special Collections.)

Once again, in 1909, Joseph Battell's largesse made more land available to expand the women's North Campus and add momentum to one of his pet projects. A potential donor, Dr. D.K. Pearsons of Chicago, was another believer in both religion and coeducation. In a letter he wrote, which the president read aloud to the faculty, Pearsons asks, among other things, what church controlled the college and warned that he had only one way of doing business. Apparently, he liked the college's response. When Pearsons Hall was completed in 1911, the site of a once dilapidated and neglected part of town had a modern showpiece dormitory with magnificent views of two mountain ranges. (Courtesy of Middlebury College Special Collections.)

When it became clear that the college's science facilities had once again become cramped and inefficient, Voter Hall was erected as the chemistry building in 1912–1913. In front of it is one of the more-level spots on campus, which naturally offered possibilities as an informal skating rink. Students jokingly called it "Rockefeller Center" after the famous rink in New York City. (Courtesy of Middlebury College Special Collections.)

The School of German was Middlebury College's first summer immersion program. It opened in 1915. Since then, the college has added 10 additional languages to its summer school repertoire: Arabic, Mandarin Chinese, French, Hebrew, Italian, Japanese, Korean, Portuguese, Russian, and Spanish. All summer language students sign a pledge to only speak the target language during the duration of the courses. Here, in 1955, German school students are dancing on the grass with Pearsons Hall and Adirondack House in the background. (Courtesy of the Werner Neuse family.)

One prominent symbol of the language programs on campus is Le Château, the cornerstone of which was laid on Bastille Day, July 14, 1924. The design was inspired by the 17th-century lodge built for Henri IV at Fontainebleau, the traditional hunting preserve of the kings of France. Its yellow-green stucco is set off by tapestry brick trim and French windows. It provided accommodations for 40 women, classrooms, a library, a parlor, offices, and a dining room. (Courtesy of Middlebury College Special Collections.)

The third and final Battell Hall was built on the North Campus on land donated by Joseph Battell. Unlike the first two wooden repurposed and renamed structures, the stone dormitory was constructed in 1950 in two stages. The two wings were united in 1955 with the addition of a central section, complete with a cupola. (Courtesy of Middlebury College Special Collections.)

Jessica Swift, as Middlebury's grande dame, was invited to participate in the installation of the cornerstone for Stewart Hall, seen here. Among those representing the college on that occasion in 1957 were three veterans of World War II: Chaplain Charlie Scott (who served in the Navy and is pictured directly behind Swift), Gordon Perine (Marine Corps), and Fred Neuberger (Army 10th Mountain Division). (Courtesy of Middlebury College Special Collections.)

After Middlebury's ski area moved in 1934 from Chipman Hill to the Snow Bowl in Hancock, enthusiasm for skiing remained strong. When Stewart Hall was opened as a dormitory for 150 men, each double room featured its own ski rack. The façade of the building was faced with native stone, and the interior included a carpeted and soundproofed study lounge. (Courtesy of Middlebury College Special Collections.)

Middlebury's Winter Carnival is believed to be the oldest student-run winter carnival in the country. In addition to ski jumping, snowshoe and obstacle races were held on Storrs Avenue. Here, viewers dressed in raccoon fur coats and fedoras watch athletes soar through the air during a winter carnival on Chipman Hill in the 1920s. Raccoon coats became so popular that George Olsen released a recording highlighting the trend called "Doin' the Raccoon": "College men, knowledge men, / Do a dance called raccoon; / It's the craze, nowadays, / And it will get you soon. / Buy a coat and try it, / I'll bet you'll be a riot, / It's a wow, learn to do it right now!"

A sleigh ride on campus was a chance to be seen. This group was prepared with stylish hats and horses of dramatically contrasting colors. In the background are Painter Hall and Old Chapel, barely visible through the branches.

Horace Fairbanks was the scion of a famous St. Johnsbury dynasty. Fairbanks served for two years as governor of Vermont. Midpoint in his term, he decided to have a handsome house and barn combination built at 7 South Street in Middlebury. Current European styles were exerting their influence. Napoleon III's hopefully named Second Empire had managed to produce its distinctive architectural legacy of Mansard roofs and Italianate scrollwork. That design was interpreted by a New York firm in 1915, and the result was what is now the Fletcher House. The house became the home of the SLUG fraternity until the college abolished the Greek system in 1991.

Coming of age during the Depression had challenged and tempered these young men. Pledging themselves to become brothers of a fraternity provided them with a sense of belonging and of collective identity. They sang songs like "A Chi Psi Went Meandering" and "Rolling, Rolling Home," but times were hard, and violence was making a regular appearance in newspaper headlines and on the radio. Kneeling at far left is Howard Munford (father of the author), who played in a dance band and referred to his standup bass as a "bull fiddle." He served on an aircraft carrier in the Pacific. Dr. Munford returned to Middlebury as a professor of American literature. His old fraternity (ΧΨ) is now named the Munford House. (Author's collection.)

The first chapter of Delta Kappa Epsilon was founded at Yale in 1854 out of "disaffection" with fraternity culture. Their pledge was one of "dignity, self-respect and morality." Middlebury College followed the same pattern, and in 1905, ΔKE brothers banded together in Painter Hall to pledge against drunken misbehavior. Later, they had their own separate house.

The fraternity system at Middlebury prompted another defection in 1905, for many of the same reasons. In that year, 10 "neutrals," male students not associated with Greek life, formed Kappa Delta Rho (ΚΔΡ) as a direct reaction against "pranks, drunkenness and elitism allowed by other fraternities." The fraternity men built this snow sculpture for Middlebury College's winter carnival in front of their house.

Six years after Middlebury began to admit women, the first sorority was organized, and every Middlebury woman was a member of Alpha Chi (AX). The sorority encouraged its young members to achieve high scholarship and provide philanthropic service to the community. In 1923, Alpha Chi transitioned to the Gamma Lambda chapter of the fraternity Kappa Kappa Gamma (ΚΚΓ). In 1934, there was enough general unhappiness that 158 out of 194 women enrolled at Middlebury signed a petition and submitted it to President Moody. They wanted sororities abolished on the grounds that the system had been arbitrarily forced onto the women to justify "equality" between the genders and thus validate the fraternities. In this photograph, the sorority sisters are studying in "the Brown Room," won after petitioning the administration for their own place on campus to pursue their studies. (Courtesy of Middlebury College Special Collections.)

Despite the groundbreaking precedent set by Emma Willard, the status quo remained stubborn, and the even earlier admonition of Mary Wollstonecraft that "minds have no sex" was slow to be officially recognized. Finally, Middlebury College admitted three women in 1883, one of whom was May Belle Chellis. She was the college's first female graduate in 1886, after forcing the trustees to grudgingly admit that two separate curricula were not needed. She proved her point by achieving the highest ranking in Greek her freshman year and being admitted to Phi Beta Kappa. (Courtesy of Middlebury College Special Collections.)

Mary Annette Anderson was born on a farm in Shoreham, Vermont, to William Anderson, a former slave, and his wife, Philomine Langlois, of Native American and French heritage. She was the first woman of color to graduate from Middlebury College. Anderson was inducted into the Phi Beta Kappa honor society, graduated as valedictorian in 1899, and was selected to deliver the commencement address. (Courtesy of Middlebury College Special Collections.)

This group of female students from the class of 1893 might have been aware of the statement by suffragist Kate Sheppard in an 1892 pamphlet: "All that separates . . . race, class, creed or sex, is inhuman, and must be overcome." At any rate, coeducation seems to have been an aid to romance, as two couples pictured here were married after graduation.

In what had become a college tradition, the author's parents met while they were students at Middlebury. Marion Jones, class of 1932, leaves Mead Chapel as Mrs. Howard Munford on September 1, 1934. They later made their home on South Street. (Courtesy of Martha Munford.)

Arthur Healey graduated from Princeton in 1926 with an MFA in architecture. In 1929, he came to Middlebury and applied his architectural talents by restoring houses, churches, and schools. When he shifted to painting, he taught at the college and became chairman of the Fine Arts Department. He never liked being called "professor." That, he would explain, was the title of "the piano player in a bordello." Social class meant nothing to him.

Healey was a bird hunter and a fisherman. For this and many other reasons, Vermonters took to him. He had many friends, including Storrs Lee, with whom he re-opened the padlocked and neglected Sheldon Museum. Many of his watercolors are there, in the Middlebury College Library, the Bennington Museum, the Museum of Fine Arts in Boston, and Harvard University's Fogg Museum. Here, he is pictured with his hunting dog Nebuchadnezzar.

When Middlebury's old wooden academy building was razed in 1867, the spot where it stood became Storrs Park. The park was later chosen as an appropriate location for the new high school, proudly dedicated in 1911. This brick structure had four massive chimneys and was centrally located enough to be within walking distance for most of its students. Fire broke out in 1954, and the building was badly damaged. The lower floors were salvaged and converted for use as the town's municipal building. It served in this capacity until 2016, when it was torn down. Where it once stood is now College Park, the symbolic merging point of town and gown.

In 1936, federal funding through the New Deal became available. A recent arrival in town from New York City, architect Arthur Healy was hired to design this monumental Doric-columned entrance to the high school gym.

Shortly after fire destroyed the third floor of the high school in 1954, Middlebury College student Tom Woolsey (class of 1956) rides a scooter in a race on the lawn of his fraternity (ATΩ). The scooter itself had once belonged to a paratrooper who had taken it with him when he jumped into Normandy in June 1944. (Courtesy of Thomas Woolsey.)

Thomas S. and Lois Ann (Guernsey) Woolsey, parents-in-law of the author, were wed in Mead Chapel in February 1957. Chaplain Charlie Scott presided over the ceremony. Their wedding reception was held at the ATΩ fraternity house. Alpha Tau Omega was founded at the Virginia Military Institute, where Thomas "Stonewall" Jackson had been an instructor. As a Christian, he probably would have approved of ATΩ's founding in 1865 as a means of reconciliation between North and South through principles of Christian brotherly love. (Courtesy of Thomas Woolsey.)

Three

The Creek, Transportation, and the Railroad

In 1777, Samuel Blodgett, at his trading post on Otter Creek, was beset by a band of 200 Mohawks, who tied him to a tree and piled brush at his feet. Blodgett managed to indicate to their leader, a British officer, that he was a fellow Freemason. The trader was promptly released. The next raid to come up the creek from Lake Champlain included redcoats, Tories, and Hessians, as well as Iroquois. In early November 1778, armed *bateaux* and war canoes led by Maj. Christopher Carleton paused below the falls in Middlebury. As the raiders portaged to go upstream, they set fire to the empty blockhouse guarding the ford. Their furthest point upstream was a barn built by Col. John Chipman. Fire arrows failed to ignite the greenwood, and tomahawks were equally ineffective. Arrowheads and hacked timbers were found in the side of the barn when it was torn down in 1950. (Courtesy of Tami Munford.)

On the night of November 3, 1927, Vermont's Green Mountains were subjected to 36 hours of continuous rainfall. The results were a catastrophic flood. Streams overran their banks, buildings were dislodged, and massive dams of debris piled up. When these dams burst, they sent 15-to-20-foot waves surging downstream into the rivers. Otter Creek roared wildly, but Middlebury was spared the fate of many other towns. Joseph Battell's stone bridge withstood the battering.

Clinton Smith's first patron was Columbus Smith (no relation) of Salisbury, who hired the fledging architect to build his palatial home in Italianate style. Columbus Smith motored north on Otter Creek in this sleek 1880 steam launch named *General Custer* every Sunday, weather permitting, to take his family to church services at St. Stephens.

In 1805, John Warren displayed his wealth by building a lavish Federal-style house. Immediately behind the Federation Building is a sharp drop-off, sliced away by quarrying stone. This allowed for a deep basement and an even deeper sub-basement. This provided a safe stop on the Underground Railroad, as the water route to Canada was flowing less than a hundred yards away. The building is now home to the Vermont Folklife Center.

The building with the cupola is Middlebury's cotton mill. It stood six stories high on the north bank of Otter Creek just below the falls. It was first built in 1811, then enlarged by David Page in 1817. He installed 20 power looms and gas lights to enable longer working hours. By 1850, boasting 100 looms, it was the biggest factory in Vermont. Female workers from small towns, supervised by male foremen, worked up to 14 hours a day, earning $3 a week. In a bit of historical irony, the cotton was supplied by slave labor, yet Vermont had the North's highest per capita volunteer enlistment in the Civil War.

Originally the site of a gristmill, the Frog Hollow Stone Mill was erected in 1840 and was listed in the National Register of Historic Places in 1973. It is a sturdy reminder of the town's industrial past. Now it is owned by Middlebury College, which uses it as a student art space.

This group of workmen are taking advantage of the snow in the winter of 1901 to maneuver what appears to be a boiler down the slope of Mill Street in Frog Hollow. Their equipment includes a block and tackle, and the muscle power is provided by a horse.

Clinton Smith referred to his business as "Number One Mill Street." It was a casualty of the fire of 1891, but was later rebuilt and is seen here in the winter of 1954. Once the industrial function of Frog Hollow became outmoded, its central location rendered it attractive to art and craft galleries and other shops. (Courtesy of Thomas Woolsey.)

Middlebury owes its existence and much of its prosperity to Otter Creek. As enterprises began to thrive on both banks, the north end of town seized the upper hand in both finance and influence. Here, the Yale-educated lawyers staked their claims in alliance with Gamaliel Painter. On the south side, the Foote clan constructed a sawmill and resented the aristocracy on the other side of the ford. One of the few things "north-enders" and "south-enders" could agree upon was the need for a bridge. The Foote contingent provided the lumber, and Gamaliel Painter the engineering skills.

The wooden bridge survived through a variety of versions and renovations until late in the 19th century. Then fire consumed the largest cotton mill and a portion of downtown, taking much of the bridge with it. Joseph Battell was a generous benefactor, but he also had very strong opinions as to how his donations should be applied. He had witnessed a series of fires, including the major conflagration of 1891. The new bridge would bear his name, and as a result, his specifications were non-negotiable. Here, a year after the cotton mill fire, the forms that would support the fireproof stone span can be seen.

A privilege of young 19th-century Americans of a certain social class was to experience the Grand Tour. Joseph Battell took a sabbatical from Middlebury College to visit Europe and returned home, especially impressed by the architecture of Rome. His new bridge paid homage to the Imperial City and its bridge spanning the Tiber River in front of the Castel Sant'Angelo. The design called for an exact duplicate of the bridge in Rome; each arch would be exactly 40 by 40 by 40 feet, but Battell was willing to forgo the elaborate sculptural decorations of the original. The plan for three classical Roman arches, even undecorated by statues, still seemed exotic to the town leaders. Joseph Battell made his position clear. After all, he was paying for over half of it. The Battell Bridge opened to traffic in 1905.

Vermont is notable for its historic covered bridges. The pulp mill itself is long gone, but the eponymous bridge is still in use, though its Burr arch design has been upgraded to two lanes with King post trusses. The bridge crosses Otter Creek on Seymour Street just downstream of Main Street on the way to Weybridge. Listed in the National Register of Historic Places in 1974, it is one of the oldest covered bridges in the country and the oldest in Vermont. The postcard view above of the one-lane bridge was sent in 1912 with a penny postage stamp. (Above, author's collection; below, courtesy of Middlebury College Special Collections.)

At the point where the Middlebury River flows into Otter Creek, the Three Mile Bridge connected the east and west banks. The story went that Seely Reynolds had problems getting his hay wagons through this narrow interior passage. Many people blamed Reynolds for the fire that destroyed the bridge in 1949. Allegedly, his reasoning was that if the bridge were to be rebuilt wider, his hay transportation problems would be over. Taken in 1948, these were the last photographs of The Three Mile Bridge. It was never replaced, much to Reynolds's chagrin. On his deathbed years later, Reynolds was asked to confess to his act of arson. "I didn't do it," he growled, "but I know who did." He took his secret with him to the grave.

Smith and Allen described their shop as "the first door on Mill Street," producing building materials for a myriad of Middlebury's important structures. Imports were kept to a minimum since marble and wood were locally available. Slate was quarried not far to the south. Clinton Smith also used the larger marble industry in Proctor, Vermont. Here, the shop, with its distinctive brick kiln chimney, takes a break from its busy schedule for a group portrait of owners and workers, including their Percheron draft horse Old Tom.

On the east bank of Otter Creek were the freight depot and the town icehouse. In winter, blocks from the ice harvest were stored here, and perishables such as milk were loaded into refrigerated freight cars. In the summer, the icehouse doubled as a boathouse for rowboats, canoes, and steam launches.

The old joke among ice cutters involved a flip of a coin, with the loser assigned to man the lower end of the saw. Local farmers generally did most of the ice harvesting.

The square chunks of ice, called "cakes," would be hauled out of Otter Creek with large ice tongs and loaded onto a wagon. The ice would then be stored in cork-insulated icehouses, with layers of sawdust packed between the blocks. Ice companies provided door-to-door delivery from icehouse to kitchen iceboxes.

After the first wooden railway bridge of 1849 on Otter Creek in Middlebury burned, it was replaced in 1860 by an old-fashioned wooden covered bridge supported by log pilings. When the railroad bridge had to be rebuilt, more modern methods and materials were used. The new trestle was bolted together out of steel girders, and its bulkhead foundations were poured concrete. The only wood used in its 1898 construction was in the railroad ties. Both the college and the town had boathouses, and here, a rowboat enjoys the placid creek.

On May 5, 1893, at 4:40 a.m., a train wreck demolished the railroad bridge at the bottom of Water Street. The crash was so loud that it woke residents as far away as South Street. Although a train full of passengers had just crossed the bridge, thankfully, there were no injuries. This view shows a group of men on the north bank assessing the damage, while a group of boys clamber over the derailed cars. The trestle was quickly rebuilt but collapsed again four days later.

On the morning of August 3, 1923, Calvin Coolidge received word that he was president while visiting family in Vermont. Two years later, President Coolidge took advantage of the "whistle stop" system to pay a visit to Middlebury. He and his wife greeted well-wishers from the platform of the rearmost car. The Rutland Railroad provided passenger service to and from Middlebury until the early 1960s.

The railroad depot, originally on Water Street, was replaced in 1891 by the Seymour Street station. Once railroad passengers arrived in town, they needed transportation. Although their vehicles are not specifically identified as taxicabs, the drivers are parked purposefully in front of the depot in new automobiles provided by Middlebury Motors.

The railroad had a depot for passenger service and another for freight, located on the southern edge of town. These were the days of the steam locomotive, and a wooden slatted water tower is looming in the background.

Steam locomotives were identified by number, and frequently pulled well-known trains. In May 1942, the *Green Mountain Flyer* arrived in town powered by Engine No. 64, "Pacific." Far away, in the actual Pacific Ocean at that point in time, Japanese and American aircraft carriers were dueling in the Battle of the Coral Sea.

In 1947, World War II veterans were coming to Vermont, many of them to attend college thanks to the GI Bill. Some undoubtedly arrived by train, such as this one pulling into Middlebury.

In order to keep up with the rest of the world, Middlebury needed an airport. A parcel of land to the east of town was flat, available, and had dimensions suitable for a runway. By 1930, hangars and other essential features were in place, making it possible to serve multiple aircraft. This is Middlebury College's flying class in 1939. (Courtesy of Middlebury College Special Collections.)

Four

The Marble Industry

In 1803, Dr. Eben Judd leased land adjacent to Otter Creek falls, built a dam across the creek, and began to quarry stone at Vermont's first mechanized marble mill. By 1811, he was shipping his marble products to Boston, Troy, Albany, New York City, New Hampshire, Montreal, and London. His products even made their way from Canada to Georgia and west via the Erie Canal. The mill annually processed between 5,000 and 10,000 square feet of slabs for tombstones, curriers' tables, mantels, stoves, sideboards, sinks, door and window caps, jambs, sills, and belt courses, but his specialty was marble chimneypieces. In 1913, a photographer climbed the steeple of the Congregational church to take this encompassing photograph showing the extent of Middlebury's marble processing enterprise.

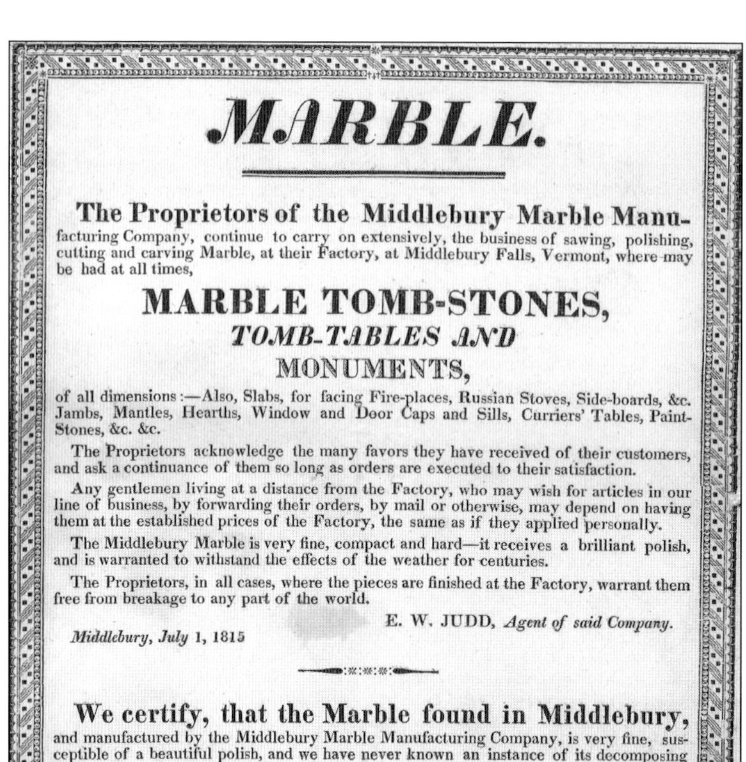

MARBLE.

The Proprietors of the Middlebury Marble Manufacturing Company, continue to carry on extensively, the business of sawing, polishing, cutting and carving Marble, at their Factory, at Middlebury Falls, Vermont, where may be had at all times,

MARBLE TOMB-STONES,
TOMB-TABLES AND
MONUMENTS,

of all dimensions:—Also, Slabs, for facing Fire-places, Russian Stoves, Side-boards, &c. Jambs, Mantles, Hearths, Window and Door Caps and Sills, Curriers' Tables, Paint-Stones, &c. &c.

The Proprietors acknowledge the many favors they have received of their customers, and ask a continuance of them so long as orders are executed to their satisfaction.

Any gentlemen living at a distance from the Factory, who may wish for articles in our line of business, by forwarding their orders, by mail or otherwise, may depend on having them at the established prices of the Factory, the same as if they applied personally.

The Middlebury Marble is very fine, compact and hard—it receives a brilliant polish, and is warranted to withstand the effects of the weather for centuries.

The Proprietors, in all cases, where the pieces are finished at the Factory, warrant them free from breakage to any part of the world.

E. W. JUDD, *Agent of said Company.*

Middlebury, July 1, 1815

We certify, that the Marble found in Middlebury, and manufactured by the Middlebury Marble Manufacturing Company, is very fine, susceptible of a beautiful polish, and we have never known an instance of its decomposing by the action of the air or water.

H. DAVIS, *President.*
F. HALL, *Prof. Math. & Nat. Phil.*
JOHN HOUGH, *Prof. Languages.*
JOEL H. LINSLEY, *Tutor.*

Middlebury College, June 30, 1815.

WM. SLADE, JUN'S PRINT—MIDDLEBURY.

This advertisement from 1815 indicates that the town took advantage of its resources from an early date. The wording demonstrates a justifiable pride in local products. By 1822, ingenious local inventors had perfected harnessing waterpower to drive marble cutting saws. The design was successful enough to secure a patent, and became a national prototype.

In the foreground, the falls remain the same, but the steel tower on the left is evidence of changing times. Electric energy has either supplemented or replaced waterpower at the marble works. The electricity-powered machines used stiff leather sprinkled with emery and rubbed the marble surfaces with old felt hats to polish it. (Courtesy of Middlebury College Special Collections.)

The southern and eastern sections of Vermont have deposits of marble in a band reaching from the Massachusetts border to Middlebury. Dr. Judd foresaw the possibilities and secured a 999-year lease from Appleton Foote to "dig marble on any part of his lot between his house and the creek, and the privilege of erecting a mill." Quarrying went on in the town itself and at points to the north and east. As late as 1942, Quarry No. 5 on Quarry Road was still active less than a mile from downtown.

Even though the Belden's Falls Company's quarry was located near the tracks, a horse and wagon were still being used to haul the slabs to the branch railroad. This marble was no ordinary product. The prominent Victorian-era sculptor Richard Greenough flatly proclaimed it, "The only marble in this country that I am yet acquainted with fit for the purposes of sculpture." He later went on to state, "I prefer it to any marble I have ever used, and I have always worked in the best marble of Carrara." High praise indeed, as Michelangelo himself worked exclusively with Carrara stone.

Although situated in Middlebury, the firm in charge of the marble industry was the Brandon Italian Marble Company. Before power machinery came along, expertise with cribbing made from wooden beams was needed to support blocks, tackles, and other lifting mechanisms. Blacksmiths were crucial to the success of the operation, and here, they stand in their forge aprons, bracketing the group of workers.

Marble quarriers were skilled professionals and justifiably proud of their status within the trade. Both precision and safety were paramount, as they worked with sledgehammers, crowbars, pickaxes, diamond-tipped drill bits, explosives, and extremely heavy weights.

Mechanical cranes made the process of hauling marble more efficient. Even then, workers were reluctant to abandon their horses completely. These workers are typical of Middlebury's interest in the future and modernization, as well as the understandable desire to hang on to long-standing traditions.

Once Middlebury's own supply of marble was largely depleted, emphasis shifted to processing and finishing the stone. This photograph shows a shop interior with its specialized equipment and the experts who ran it.

Not far from this entrance to the Halpin Falls Bridge was the Marble Ledge, leased by the Old Middlebury or Cutter Quarrying Company. From 1850 to 1925, a mill served the quarry and was an important contributor to the local marble industry. It offered "Sawed Marble caps and sills, Tombstones, Monuments, &c. &c."

Also known as the "High Covered Bridge," the 66-foot long lattice through-truss covered bridge over the Muddy Branch of the New Haven River is, at 41 feet above the riverbed, the highest covered bridge in the state. The Halpin Falls Bridge was listed in the National Register of Historic Places in 1974. Built in 1824, a marble quarry was located below the falls, and a holding pond fed a water wheel to power the marble cutting saws.

Five

Public Gatherings, Parades, and Entertainment

The layout of Middlebury's streets is such that processions could approach the center of town from either north or south, and photographers had an advance warning to select a vantage point from a third-floor window or even a flat roof. This view is to the north up Main Street. The Republican Party is celebrating the 1888 victory of Benjamin Harrison over Grover Cleveland. The Allen Block in the right background was destroyed in the fire of 1891.

In the 1890s, the national spirit was one of expansion and preparation for the world stage. This military parade includes plumes and other martial trappings as they proceed along Merchants' Row.

Regalia and uniforms complemented one another as public spectacle. Here, members of a fraternal organization are resplendent as they pass the high school. The year is 1924.

Flags were flying and a feeling of celebration was in the air as Middlebury declared enthusiasm for Pres. Ulysses S. Grant and his vice president, Henry Wilson. Whenever Main Street was free of snow, it was parade season.

Vermont has always loved its oxen, so star teams competed at the fair, heaving into their hand-carved yokes at the commands of "Gee!" and "Haw!" as they strained to move huge weights. It was their job, and they had their own celebrity. A man was judged by the condition as well as the performance of his animals.

Vermont fairs, although their numbers have dwindled, remain a seasonal event anticipating autumn and the harvest. Girls in pinafores, boys on bicycles, and men in derby hats gathered to view the spectacles arriving in town. During the heyday of the circus, the local fairgrounds were a logical place for the tents to be set up. Here, the usual sight of animals on Main Street was made unusual by the stately appearance of an elephant.

In order to share his passion for fine horses, Col. Silas Ilsley paid for the creation of the Addison County Fairgrounds, complete with racetrack and covered grandstands. Shown here is the entrance on Court Street, featuring the recycled former courthouse.

This scene is rich with buggies and shays, the women resplendent with long sleeves, longer dresses, and ankle-length skirts. Every person in sight is wearing a hat. The headgear is elaborate for the ladies, solidly respectable for the men. The new century has had nine years to create a new status quo. Perhaps because it is Vermont, the changes have not quite caught up yet.

Harness racing involves trotting and pacing horses pulling a light, two-wheeled vehicle called a sulky. The origins of the sport go back to ancient Assyria and Egyptian royalty when chariots were used, first in war and later in lion hunting. Races usually covered a mile and a quarter around a circular track. The October 1911 issue of *The Vermonter* magazine featured a special report of the Addison County Fair with this photograph, captioned, "The Middlebury Way. A fair field, a fine track, two bands, careful policing, every seat and point of vantage taken, and money in the bank. What more could one ask?"

As seen by this photograph of the fairgrounds parking lot jammed with cars, automobiles were becoming the wave of the future. To the dismay of Joseph Battell, car races would soon become as popular as horse racing.

The decades following World War I saw the United States gripped by aviation fever. Coming home, many former military pilots found a new use for their skills and flew from one county fair to another, performing daredevil stunts and "barnstorming."

Six

The Town's Architect, Victorian Middlebury, and Downtown

An exemplar of the Victorian era's optimistic energies, Clinton Smith left his architectural stamp on Middlebury and beyond. He was born on a local farm in 1846. He recovered from typhoid at age 14 and apprenticed himself to a builder, quickly mastering the trade. His first commission was a mansion named Shard Villa in Salisbury. Having established his reputation, he partnered with William Allen and proceeded to transform his hometown, designing the Beckwith Block, courthouse, and Methodist church, among others. His grave in the Foote Street Cemetery is marked by a statue of a grieving angel.

In this view from across the creek, the town hall designed by Clinton Smith is clearly recognizable. Just south of it is the architect's home, and below it is his carriage house. The main floor of the house faces South Pleasant Street and stands at the same elevation as the town hall. On the creek side, however, the ground drops away sharply enough to the west for the white wooden railing and slate roof of the second-story porch to wrap around the southwest corner and become part of the first floor.

Framing the big double doorway facing north are two slim white marble columns, which serve to punctuate and visually anchor the Romanesque arch. The town hall's tapered keystone is also white marble, and the variegation provided by white spacer blocks suggests the Moorish arches seen in the mosques and palaces of Spain. White marble bands divide the brick facade and run horizontally, visually tying the tower together with the central hall itself. Currently, this venue houses the Town Hall Theater.

In an all-too-familiar scenario, Middlebury's original Methodist church, first constructed in 1837, burned down in the conflagration-plagued year of 1891, adding one more casualty to the list of 11 buildings and the wooden bridge lost downtown.

When the Methodist church was replaced, native son architect Clinton Smith was given what would be one of his last jobs in Middlebury. The square bell tower could be home to a Renaissance prince. Although Smith was very fond of Romanesque lines, in this case, only the entrances have them, while the main windows are framed by double, if subtle, Gothic arches.

At far left is one of the most elaborately detailed buildings in Middlebury. Built in 1882–1883, the Beckwith Block was the first big public commission for local architect Clinton Smith. The masonry is quite extraordinary in its details, featuring terra-cotta, stone, and lavish brickwork, all crowned with an eye-catching cornice. It became enough of a source of local pride to ensure Smith a series of other important jobs. Beckwith & Company sold cloth, rugs, and notions from the building, where a dentist also had an office.

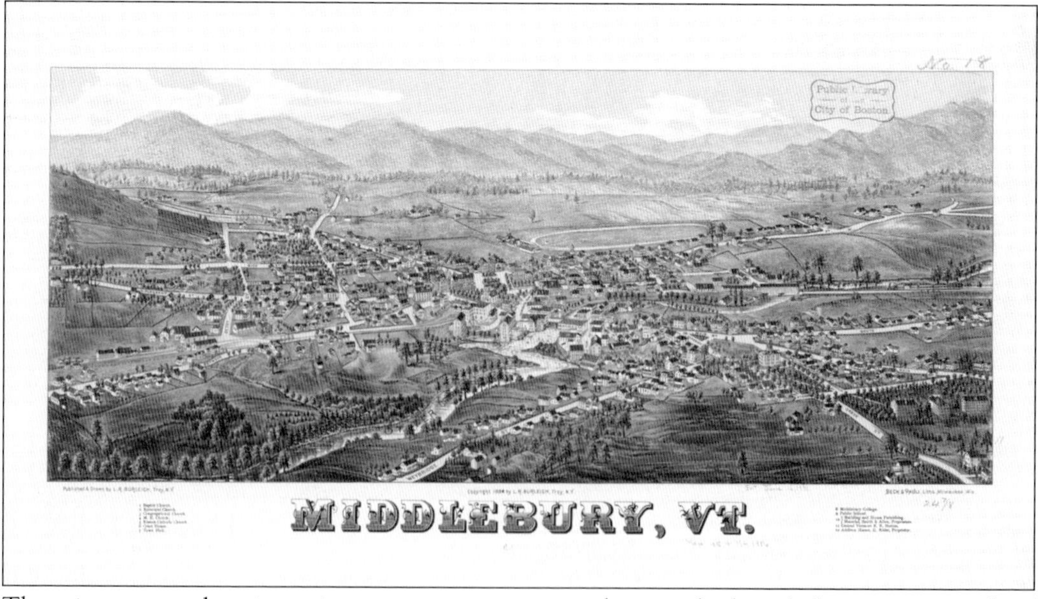

There is an art and a science in presenting a conjectural view, which includes a precise study of maps and an understanding of trigonometry. This 1886 Victorian-era lithograph by Lucien Burleigh presents a remarkably accurate view of the town and its main streets, looking east toward the Green Mountains. L.R. Burleigh's company in Troy, New York, produced such views of around 280 locations and at least 163 panoramic city plans.

Joseph Battell's niece Anna Jessica Stewart was born in the same house as her famous uncle. Much later in her very long life, in the philanthropic tradition of the family, she donated the building to the town. When she was five, she moved to what is now the Swift House Inn. In her 20s, she fell in love with the young and impecunious Rev. Walter Sylvester. Her father did not approve, and they were kept apart for years until he was diagnosed with consumption. At that point, the young couple eloped, and she took care of him until he died a year later.

In 1913, Jessica Stewart married again, this time with her father's approval. Charles Swift was a man of considerable and widespread business interests. She accompanied him on his worldwide travels until his death in 1929. Upon returning to Middlebury, Jessica resumed her Sunday spot in the Congregational church, sitting in the Battell Pew, No. 23. Since Chipman Hill's ski slope and jump were not far from her home on High Street, she went to watch winter carnival, along with (from left to right) Colonel MacLane, John Machs, and Miss Selkin. The last of Middlebury's great philanthropists died at the age of 110, having managed to be the oldest person to ever fly in an airplane.

Joseph Battell was born in the home built by Horatio Seymour. By the time of his death in 1915, from the Battell Block and Bridge downtown to the Breadloaf Campus in Ripton and the Morgan Horse Farm in Weybridge, Battell left his mark. He owned a newspaper, *The Middlebury Register*, and, as a dedicated horseman, penned editorials against the emergent automobile. He also self-published an ambitious tome in two volumes: *Ellen, Or the Whisperings of an Old Pine*, an eccentric work combining druidic animism, with an ongoing critique of science, philosophy, and wide-ranging mathematical speculation.

The Battell Block replaced what had been five previous buildings along that section of creek bank. The tower, complete with a conical roof, was damaged beyond repair by the hurricane of 1950 and never replaced.

In this view looking toward the Battell Block, two local establishments bracket Main Street. On the right is Pine Hall, where Frank Bond ran a roller-skating rink, until the fad died out and he converted the space to a haberdashery. Opposite is the China Hall, where B.F. Wales, an optician, sold jewelry, watches, crockery, and also china. It is mud season in downtown Middlebury.

At the turn of the 20th century, electricity had come to stay, and electric power lines zigzagged like spiderwebs above Main Street. The original turret on the Battell Block in the background caps the apartment of Joseph Battell himself, where he used his telescope to keep an eye on his beloved town.

Silas Ilsey, a veteran of the Civil War and a success in the lucrative tin business, settled in Middlebury with his wife. As laconic as Battell was effusive, Colonel Ilsley set himself to be one of his adopted town's major benefactors. He provided funding for a Baptist church and a war memorial. Ilsley, as Battell had been, was generous to Middlebury College. It says something about the man that the only detailed document Colonel Ilsley left behind was his will, providing handsomely for his head groom. (Courtesy of Ilsley National Bank of Middlebury.)

In 1848, a group of men formed a reading group that referred to itself as the Middlebury Lyceum. In 1866, sixty women signed articles to officially form the Ladies Library Association. A year later, men were admitted. The library continued to function in cramped quarters over a bank. Silas Ilsley came to the rescue, bequeathing a sum of $25,000 for a library, an amount matched by his widow. The library was completed in 1924 in the Classical style, intentionally representing a temple of learning. In 1977 and 1989, additions were made to accommodate steadily increasing demands. (Author's collection.)

As the commander of two regiments during the Civil War, Col. Ilsley led his men from horseback. As a civilian, he could afford his own stable. This shot of Washington Street shows his livery on the right. In front of it, a huge mastiff guards his territory. (Courtesy of Middlebury College Special Collections.)

Photographers were quick to explore and experiment with their medium, and in the age of charades and *tableaux vivants*, the potential for theater had opened up as well. The owner and proprietor of Jackson Studios, in this double self-portrait, "Jackson Insulting Himself," manages to share the joke with his public. Even as early as 1906, Jackson gently reminds the viewer that a photograph should not always be trusted to tell the truth.

Probably embellished in the 1920s, the artist has let imagination fly as well as a wild assortment of blimps and balloons. The railroad's passenger service has likewise been elevated, but Main Street itself remains unpaved.

As proof that photographs have been subject to alteration for a long time, this 1910 "stand alone" portrait of the newly completed National Bank cannot be replicated without causing the taller brick structures to both north and south to vanish. A Burlington architect, F.L. Austin, had been brought in as part of the wave of architectural fashion promoted by the Chicago World's Columbian Exposition in 1893, proving once again that Greek Revival was not going away. Even without photo manipulation, the National Bank of Middlebury needs no help in being both solidly impressive and monumentally secure; a vault within a temple is still a safe place for anyone's money. (Author's collection.)

When the railroad's path through town cut off a corner of the town green, it was labeled Triangle Park. In 1908, Joseph Battell, perhaps influenced by memories of his Grand Tour of Europe as a young man, and certainly prodded into action by Silas Ilsley's donation of the Civil War Monument in 1905, allied himself with the Century Club to decorate the diminutive park with an oversized fountain, complete with an eagle.

Joseph Battell's fountain decorates this view of Triangle Park in the mid-1930s. The train tracks are invisible, as the rail-bed runs 20 feet below the level of Main Street and Merchants' Row. The fountain, while impressive, tended to spray the vicinity on windy days. Open cars parked nearby had their upholstery soaked, and the fountain lost popularity. It was dismantled in 1938.

Henry Sheldon's family, like so many others in Middlebury, originated in Connecticut, but he was raised on a farm in Salisbury, Vermont. It was a time when handiness was valued, and young Henry distinguished himself by both building an organ and learning to play it. This talent proved useful when he moved to Middlebury and became the organist for St. Stephen's Church for 34 years. He was an observer and a disciplined writer who kept meticulous diaries. He also was a discriminating collector who started with coins and then branched out. Sheldon wanted, as any good curator would, to not only preserve but also exhibit the evidence of the past for the public to experience.

CARRIAGE USED BY PRESIDENT MONROE

Recently Took Mr Sheldon of Middlebury, Vt, on a Birthday Ride.

HENRY L. SHELDON AND AGED FRIENDS IN PRES MONROE'S CARRIAGE.

In 1829, one of downtown Middlebury's grand brick houses was built by Eben Judd with money earned from Frog Hollow marble, some of which can be seen in the porch columns. Henry Sheldon, having established himself in town, bought the house in 1875. He allowed himself two rooms to live in and dedicated the rest to the Sheldon Art Museum, Archeological and Historical Society, which opened to the public in 1882; it was the first incorporated village museum in the country. This clipping is from the September 4, 1904, *Boston Globe*.

This view of Main Street looking north toward the Congregational and Episcopal churches shows the aftermath of the great fire of 1891. It left a gap between buildings, later to be filled by Joseph Battell's fireproof block. The fire hydrant in the foreground and electric streetlights hanging overhead are Battell's improvements. The bicycle with both front and back wheels the same size indicates that the new century has arrived in Middlebury.

In 1932, federal funding became available under the Hoover administration, and a site was chosen on Main Street for a new post office. The location was occupied at the time by the wooden Brewster Block, which housed the Middlebury Fire Department. The Brewster Block was demolished, and the fire department moved around the corner to Seymour Street. The new post office was a brick and marble landmark on Main Street, opened to the public in 1933. (Courtesy of Middlebury College Special Collections.)

The winter of 1950 saw temperatures as low as 40 degrees below zero. On Middlebury's Main Street, snow-covered cars are driving by the Campus Movie Theatre, which is playing *Come Back Little Sheba* and *The Adventures of Robinson Crusoe*.

Addison County residents could read about the Korean War as well as local news in Middlebury's new *Addison Independent*, located in Printer's Alley. William J. Slator and his wife, Celine, owned Addison Press, which published the newspaper and also served as a commercial printing plant from 1946 to 1955.

Seven

From Stable to Garage

All that has endured from the horse and buggy era are the marble hitching posts with their iron rings still attached to hold the reins as well as the strategically located blocks of stone where the ladies could step up into their carriages while keeping their dignity intact. Hitching posts and a steppingstone are visible in front of this c. 1889 photograph of the Seminary Street Schoolhouse. Marble relics such as this are still scattered around town as reminders of a bygone era.

Wintertime meant sleighs and sledges. Here, a full sleigh stands in front of the Episcopal church in 1888. Perhaps the church is providing transportation to its services for parishioners.

The man driving the sleigh is Tom Chapman, and the horse's name is Fleetfoot. The building in the background houses the A.F. Styles photograph gallery. In 1861, Styles moved to Florida for his health and pioneered a new photographic technique using dry collodion photographic plates preserved with tannin. His specialty was the then-popular stereopticon photograph. A caption on the back of this photograph reads, "I had to take my dog along to keep the girls away."

This sleigh has paused in front of the courthouse on its way from the Addison House. The year is 1888, and the first Kodak cameras had just become available to the public for taking snapshots.

Once central to commercial, agricultural, and private needs, the harness shop was a thriving concern. Every piece of tack from saddles to bridles and reins was for sale or could be repaired here at Kidder's Harness Shop. Toussaint Kidder was born in Beloeil, Quebec, in 1837. He moved to Middlebury when he was 18 and ran his harness shop on Merchants' Row for over 40 years. His son George owned Kidder's, a popular restaurant and bakery on Main Street.

Murder!

Will out is an old saying; and now it has been brought to light that for **CASH**

A. B. SMITH

will during the next 30 days give a BIG DISCOUNT on his

Carriages, Buggies, Carts, Harnesses, etc.

A few reasons why he can sell cheap and why you ought to buy of him: He buys for cash and saves discounts. He has no rent to pay. He warrants them to outwear anything. He gives you better prices; don't forget it. He buys and sells on the square. He knows how to order buggies that wear well. He tells no lies to sell you. He is satisfied with a small profit. He doesn't have to divide profits. He is at home every day. He is a blacksmith and sees that everything is all right. He saves you money. In a few days he will have different styles of

CUTTERS

and will be pleased to show them to you.

A. B. SMITH, Blacksmith,

15 Washington St.,

MIDDLEBURY, VT.

As a thriving shire town, Middlebury needed a weekly newspaper. In 1836, *The People's News* and *The Anti-Masonic Democrat* appeared, only to change names six more times before 1850. In that year, *The Middlebury Register* was decided upon as a title. It featured detailed local news as well as national and global stories. From 1883 to shortly before his death in 1919, the *Register* was owned by Joseph Battell and flourished under his leadership. In its second location in the Vallette Block, the *Register* office provides an appropriate background for Battell and his beloved team of horses.

Much like its owner, the *Register's* advertising section was not averse to exclamation points and hyperbole. Once A.B. Smith had captured the reader's attention with the word "Murder!" he then reassured them that "he is a blacksmith and sees that everything is all right." The *Register* ran until 1947.

John Kenworthy had been gassed during World War I and was a resident of the Poor Farm during the Great Depression. Eventually, he was given a job and a place to stay. He had a cot in the basement of the Battell Block and was responsible for the boilers there. Twice a year, he was tackled, stripped of his coveralls, and cleaned up using a firehose and scrub brushes. Then he was given new clothes. When Kenworthy died, his personal effects included a surprising amount of cash earned by delivering groceries in a handcart. Instead of bags, in those days, parcels were wrapped with twine. Kenworthy used to like to string twine between trees on the green, and he left behind a ball of it four feet in diameter.

In contrast to Kenworthy, these 1920s dignitaries sweeping into town in their luxurious roadster have an audience of impressed children standing near Exhibition Hall on Court Street. Clearly, times have changed and speeded up as well. The journey from the big city to the country has now become a matter of hours rather than days, or even weeks.

When William Zeno's original garage burned, he relocated to what had been a one-story building housing Joseph Durrance and converted it into a garage and repair shop, this time on Court Street. In 1928, Zeno's Garage on Seminary Street was more than a filling station and repair shop. It was a haven for men, but decorum ruled, and no questionable pictures were ever on display.

This odd combination of gas pumps and Victorian architecture dated 1946 was the result of practicality on the part of William and Clara Zeno at 31 Court Street. As early as 1928, Clara had begun helping her husband by installing pumps in front of her beauty shop, Le Claire Salon de Beauté. She also sold candy, sundries, and auto supplies.

On October 24, 1927, this line of traffic is backed up on a new section of Route 7 North, waiting to head into town. The march of progress had its ups and downs.

The transition from horse and carriage to automobiles turned out to be a relatively gradual one. Proof of coexistence in downtown Middlebury as late as the 1940s is provided by this sign on the western edge of the green near St. Stephen's, reserving a section of parking spaces for horses. It was the era of gasoline rationing, and for some rural citizens, the old means of transport must have made sense.

On their way to the Addison County Fair, Ellis and Philo Foster, along with Seely Reynolds, pose with their teams of oxen. The Foster family later founded a prominent garage and car dealership. Seely Reynolds became a manager in the local marble industry and a lister for the town.

In 1940, Foster's Socony garage was of modest size with one anonymous mechanic. Later, Foster Motors was forced to move to the edge of town in order to have room to expand. Despite the best efforts of Joseph Battell, the automobile was in Middlebury to stay.

Eight

Churches, Main Streets, Businesses, and Hotels

Although Joseph Battell would not have appreciated the takeover of his beloved town by the hated automobile, he might have been reassured by how much of the northern view of Main Street from his Battell Block tower apartments had remained the same. Although Battell died in 1919 and did not see the building of the new post office, he was not opposed to progress as such and would have understood that Middlebury needed to keep in touch with the rest of the world.

As part of the architectural legacy left behind by Smith and Allen, Middlebury's first Baptist church was built on Merchants' Row in 1882 for $8,000. The designer's fondness for decoration can be seen in the elaborate shingle and slate work.

What drew Silas Ilsley to Middlebury is not clear, but his father, a Baptist minister, had been assigned to Bridport sometime before the Civil War. As one of Colonel Ilsley's philanthropic gestures, he provided funding for the Romanesque-style towered stone Memorial Baptist Church on South Pleasant Street, constructed in 1905. Handsome stained-glass windows grace the apse of the church.

Catholic Church, Middlebury, Vt.

Despite their longer history in the Champlain Valley, in the 19th century, the town's Roman Catholics remained a minority, and a French Canadian one at that. As a result, Saint Mary's was one of the last of Middlebury's churches to be built. By 1907, under the encouragement of an enthusiastic young monsignor, the work was completed.

William Henry Porter was born to a struggling Middlebury farm family in 1861. When the farm failed, they relocated to Saratoga Springs. As a young man, he obtained a job working at an inn. Noticed by a wealthy guest, he was offered a position at a New York City bank in 1878. Eventually, after he became very wealthy, Porter served on the board of trustees at Middlebury College. The college needed an infirmary, and the town lacked a hospital. Porter donated $50,000, rolling both needs into one, the only gentle caveat being that the building "would face to the Northeast and . . . that wonderful view of the Green Mountains." The hospital opened in 1925.

The 19th century was not one for euphemism when it came to certain realities. Funeral parlors and funeral directors had yet to be invented. In 1873, Main Street was a logical place to offer "Readymade Coffins" (sign just visible behind the foliage), and the local livery stable was always available to supply a pre-draped hearse to be pulled by two black horses through the gates of Middlebury's West Cemetery.

A.J. Blackmer was Middlebury's most prominent undertaker at the turn of the 20th century. In the May 8, 1903, issue of *The Middlebury Register*, Blackmer advertised, "A new stock of coffins, caskets, etc., has been received and I am prepared to answer calls day or night promptly." He also repaired and sold furniture in the same venue. In 1911, H.D. Archer took over the building in the Register Block on Main Street to open a harness and repair shop.

Through this entrance to the West Cemetery, mourners would come as a slow-moving stream of black following the horse-drawn hearse. Middlebury citizens, provided they were Protestants, had the comfort of knowing they could end up here. Family plots are symbolic territory, a form of permanent settlement. Here lie the Painters, the Chipmans, and the Storrs. Joseph Battell and the Sheldons are, oddly enough, buried adjacent to the mummy of an Egyptian prince. Amasa Tracy, Middlebury's Civil War hero, is interred here. Many of the inscriptions provide grim evidence that infant mortality and death during childbirth were brutally common in the early 19th century.

Joe Calvi's store was a longtime institution on Main Street. His soda fountain, complete with marble countertop and a back balcony overlooking Otter Creek, was especially popular with college students. This portrait of the proud Italian proprietor was made in 1902. Much as Irish workers had arrived to build the railroad, Italian families were associated with the marble-cutting workshops but diversified into other enterprises.

In 1913, Ransom S. Benedict posed with this group in front of his grocery store on Merchants' Row. From left to right are Ada Zefferman, Napoleon Boudreau, Benedict, Arthur Forest, Col. James M. Tracy, and Fred Owen.

This interior view of the store, with its tin roof and wooden flooring, shows that it was a busy and cluttered space. In the November 25, 1904, *Middlebury Register*, Benedict's Store advertised "Fresh Canned Soups . . . New Nuts, Dates, Figs, Cranberries, Crisp Malaga Grapes, Florida Oranges, Cluster Table Raisins, Shoreham Cheese, Heinz's Pickles in glass or by the quart, fine line of Confectionery, Nabisco Sugar Wafers, Festino's, etc. Notice our Worcester Salt Fire Place, and drink 'Ulike' coffee if you want the very best." (Courtesy of Middlebury College Special Collections.)

Along with deliveries of blocks of ice for their iceboxes, turn-of-the-century housewives were accustomed to receiving milk and other groceries at their doorsteps. Benedict's Store made morning and afternoon deliveries using this handsome van. The horse was named Juniper, and she was a familiar sight to many households in Middlebury in 1903.

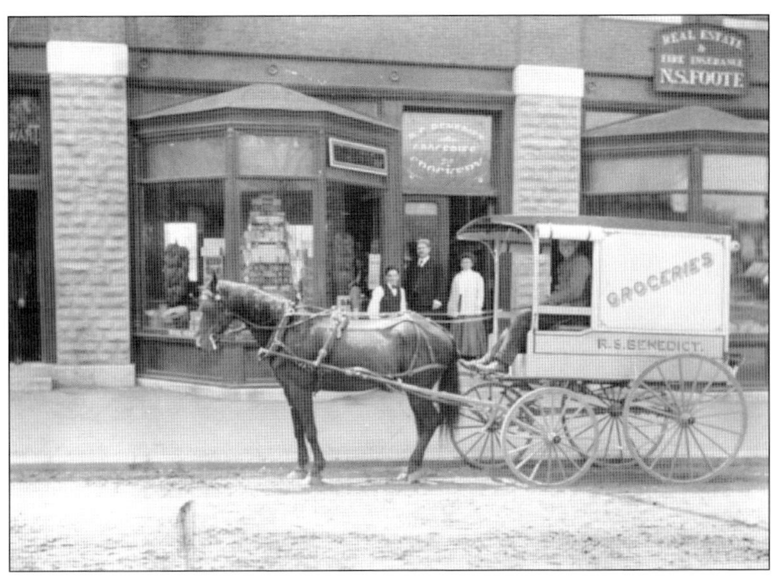

In 1926, a group of retail operators in Poughkeepsie, New York, founded the Independent Grocers Alliance (IGA). Their slogan was "Hometown Proud Supermarkets." A few years later, Marshall J. Armstrong, a farmer whose lambs and produce won many ribbons at the fair, opened an IGA supermarket in his hometown of Middlebury. Despite the Depression, the IGA store on Seymour Street has managed to secure a tempting display of produce. The store's access to the IGA supply chain helped it acquire fresh goods.

Charles Donah's market opened around 1926 and would continue to serve Washington and Seminary Street residents into the 1960s. The store sold Jumbo bread, colas, milk, cleaning products, newspapers, sliced meats, cigarettes, penny candy, donuts, fruits, and other grocery items. Notice that a 24-ounce can of peaches sold for only 15¢ and the "always cool" Campus Theater was showing a rather racy array of films, including *Damaged Lives*, *Fools for Scandal*, and *Woman Against Woman*.

On the opposite side of the street from Donah's market stood the Hotel Allen. L.O. Allen first owned a horse sales and livery business before buying the building next door and adding two stories to it to create a hotel. In 1908, C.W. Newell became the hotel's proprietor. In this 1910 scene, the hotel's blacksmith can be seen on the right in his leather apron.

According to an article in *The Middlebury Register* from May 21, 1909, "The stables connected with the Hotel Allen are the largest in the village . . . and it can be truly said that the rigs coming from these stables are the equal of any private conveyonce [sic] in this section." In this 1910 photograph, an actual surrey with fringe on the top, pulled by a handsome team of gray horses, is picking up a passenger in front of the Hotel Allen.

A number of buildings in Middlebury have had their names changed at least twice. One example is the Pierce House, which was originally the Sargent House. Whatever its title, it was a popular hostelry, especially with men of all ages. The hunting around Middlebury was good, and the hotel's cook stands ready to spring into action around 1904.

The high ground to the north of Court Square abutting the north-south Center Turnpike was always a logical spot for a hostelry. The first inn to be constructed there had Gamaliel Painter's blessing. In 1794, Samuel Mattocks had built a tavern on this prime piece of real estate, which served thirsty travelers until 1816, when it was destroyed by fire. In 1826, the Vermont House was constructed on the site and was an immediate success. In 1852, its bricks were painted yellow and a cupola was added, along with a new title: the Addison House. Colonel Ilsley and his wife lived there in a private suite until his death in 1919. By 1926, the building was in need of extensive repairs. At this point, the Treadway Inn chain purchased the building and renovated it, removing both the yellow paint and the cupola, and giving the establishment its current name: the Middlebury Inn.

Once it became common for families to have their own cars, new possibilities were opened up for vacations. Tourism flourished, along with housekeeping cabins such as this one overlooking Middlebury from the north on Route 7. A sign in front reads, "Grand View Lodge, Rooms, Cabins" and a smaller one underneath reads, "Fresh Maple Orchards candies here."

Shortly after opening its doors in 1896, Isaac Stern's Park Drug Store advertised its inventory featuring everything from "Crel Oil, best lice killer for stock" to "drugs, chemicals, confectionary, perfumery, toilet soaps and cigars." Sterns also stocked ladies' pocketbooks, stationery, postcards, and chocolates, and was the place to go "if you want a glass of good soda water" or a ticket to the opera at the town hall. Here, Sterns poses proudly with his staff in the mid-1920s. Despite the tranquility of this scene, being a druggist could be a hazardous profession. In 1915, the previous proprietor, E.A. Frost, had been badly burned on his face and hands after opening a bottle of prussic acid. Park Drug Store remained open until the mid-1990s.

This team of horses is waiting patiently on Main Street, switching their tails at the hitching post on the edge of the town green. They know the routine, which started before dawn. When their driver returns, he will deliver the cans of milk on the back of his wagon both to the freight depot icehouse and the stores on Merchants' Row. Addison County has long referred to itself as "the Land of Milk and Honey." Many dairy farms, such as those of the Butlers, Fletchers, and Pecks, operated within the town.

During the 1950s, Vermont had more cows than people, and dairy products were plentiful. One result, made possible by increased family mobility, was Palmers Dairy Bar.

Sandwiched between the town hall and Grace Baptist Church, the Park Diner opened in the 1930s. In this photograph, the owner, Charles Smith, serves a hungry group in 1951. The diner served good, wholesome diner fare, and was famous for its milkshakes.

Charles Smith and his brother Francis stand in front of the Park Diner in 1951. The McCarthy Era was in full swing, and Middlebury College faculty were keeping a close eye on the trial of Julius and Ethel Rosenberg, who were charged with treason after selling atomic secrets to Russia. The diner closed in June 2018 after being bought by the Town Hall Theater for additional rehearsal and storage space.

American Express began as a freight forwarding company in 1850. As international journeys became more affordable and desirable to many Americans, the company expanded its travel services and introduced the travelers' cheque in 1891. Middlebury College's summer language schools meant professors and students from around the world would travel to Middlebury and be in need of the company's services. The southern side of this store at 37 Main Street is still home to an American Express travel company.

The concept of a dollar store is not new, as this 1930s United 5¢ to $1.00 Store proves. Both china and baskets are displayed in the window. Next door is Baldwin's grocery store, and one of the lawyers from LaFleurs' law firm upstairs is taking a break.

This is Mit Brown's garage on Washington Street in 1940. Signs on the building read, "Let Us Marfax Your Dodge / Plymouth," "Emergency Calls, ALA," and "Don't Hibernate . . . Insulate! Protect your car for Winter Now." Despite the fact that there is snow on the ground, the woman filling her tank is wearing short sleeves, a testament to the toughness of Vermonters.

In November 1950, a tropical storm hit Middlebury with hurricane force. Trees went down, and there was widespread structural damage. Many college students volunteered to help with the cleanup. Wind was, however, not the only danger to Middlebury's trees.

Middlebury, like many New England towns, was once graced by its American elm trees, standing in long rows with their spreading canopies reaching out to shade the streets. These views, looking south on North Pleasant Street (above) and South Street (below), have vanished except for most of the buildings. Much as a previous blight had annihilated the once-mighty American chestnut, the elms were doomed. In 1945, the Dutch elm beetle arrived in southern Vermont, and by 1960 had made it as far north as Middlebury. Middlebury College tried to preserve its elms by eliminating the elm bark beetle.

Nine

Fires, Firefighters, Soldiers, and War

Middlebury's fire department has long been a proud institution of the town. In the 1800s, every homeowner was required to have at hand a bucket hook, a ladder capable of reaching the eaves of the house and barn, and also a 10-quart leather pail. In 1846, under the fire bylaws passed at a meeting of the corporation of the Village of Middlebury, the citizens agreed to organize a fire company to be known as the Middlebury Fire Co. No. 1. Here, the members are shown in full uniform, lined up on the green.

Throughout the 19th century, the combination of wooden buildings, coal, and wood-heating systems, plus a lack of pressurized water for firefighting, resulted in a series of devastating fires. Some proved impossible to control and had to be left to burn themselves out. Seen here are dramatic views of the devastation left behind in downtown Middlebury after the fire of 1875.

On November 23, 1891, the fire alarm went off in downtown Middlebury. A crowd of concerned citizens hurried to lend a hand. Unfortunately, the pump malfunctioned, permitting the fire to spread wildly. Four hours later, the shops on Merchants' Row were laid low. Main Street was wiped out as far as the Beckwith Block. Here are before and after views of Middlebury and the fire of 1891. Eleven buildings were completely annihilated. Shortly after the conflagration, the townspeople voted to rebuild with an iron bridge. The Battell clan was adamant that the bridge should be made of stone. They agreed that if the town would offer up the first $12,000, Joseph Battell and his father would split anything over that amount. That sealed the deal.

This dramatic scene captured on camera in 1904 makes it clear that the College Street School's bell tower is doomed. The top floor of the three-story structure was saved by the prompt action of the Middlebury Fire Department and quick access to the new firefighting water mains paid for by Joseph Battell.

The school fire of 1904 left behind an empty husk of brick walls. It was rebuilt and refurbished, but its cupola was out of style by then and was never replaced.

Despite the archaic-looking firefighting equipment, this fire on Main Street did not result in the destruction of 1891. The Battell Bridge is in evidence, which suggests Battell's modernized system of reservoirs, hydrants, and pressurized hoses were also in effect. This is most likely the fire of 1909, which destroyed the Atwood Block.

Middlebury's fire station had been attached to the Brewster Block. When that was torn down, a new station was built on Seymour Street. Here, Harold Caul and Warren Needham are standing in front of the department's 1956 Chevrolet panel truck.

At the Battle of Cedar Creek in 1864, Lt. Col. Amasa Tracy said simply, "Vermonters don't run." He held the line long enough for General Phil Sheridan on his Morgan stallion Rienzi to arrive and turn a rout into a victory. Tracy's courage won him the Medal of Honor. After the war, he became a storekeeper. (Courtesy of the Vermont Historical Society.)

Servicemen from Middlebury were killed at the battles of Savage Station, Gettysburg, and the Wilderness. Others perished in camp from disease. Col. Silas Ilsley commanded two Brooklyn regiments in the Civil War. He funded the war memorial, and when asked to speak at its dedication in 1905, he stood up and said, "I take a pleasure in presenting this monument to the soldiers of Middlebury." Then he sat down.

This detachment of cavalry is headed for the freight depot, where a train awaits both horses and equipment. With the possible exception of officers, the men will also ride in boxcars and have bales of hay for seats. The hogshead cask in the wagon on the right contains water. Judging by the men's uniforms, they are most likely heading off to fight in the Spanish American War in 1898.

Mirroring many previous scenes in the capitals of Europe three years earlier, these young Middlebury men of 1917 were marching off to fight in World War I. Europe's initial wave of enthusiasm had long since bogged down, sunk in the mud and blood of the Western Front, at the battlefields of Ypres, at Verdun, and on the Somme. America, the feeling went, had the fresh spirit and martial follow-through needed to tip the scales and break the deadlock overseas.

This outburst of military high spirits in front of the Battell Block on Main Street is shot through with relief and joy. There is something spontaneous about the knot of men in uniform who have just received great news. Is it the signing of the Armistice? At least one soldier is dancing a jig, and a rifle has turned into a prop for a gymnastic maneuver.

Standing on the green in 1985, World War I aviators William Murphy and Steven Freeman are wearing their original uniforms. Memories of poison gas, barbed wire, and machine guns lingered, but there was reason to hope that humanity had learned a valuable lesson. Freeman was a professor of French at Middlebury College, where he was a pioneer in the field of foreign language teaching. He lived to be 101 years old and died in Shard Villa. (Courtesy of Jim Peden.)

On Armistice Day 1925, Middlebury dedicated its second war memorial, a slab of granite with two bronze plaques. On the north side are the names of soldiers who fought in the Revolutionary War, Spanish American War, and World War I. The south side is reserved for the Civil War. Each fatality is marked by an asterisk.

In 1936, a northbound driver failed to negotiate the right turn around Court Square and plowed across the upper green, knocking the honor roll over. It was replaced on its pedestal and continues to document the history of generations of Middlebury's warriors, including the names not inscribed on the larger granite monument.

On November 17, 1918, Lt. Waldo Heinrichs was flying a patrol in his Nieuport 28 fighter when he was jumped by six German Fokkers. Heinrichs's guns jammed. His enemies' guns, as he remarked drily, did not. He was hit 10 times, with one bullet going through his mouth and another shattering his left arm. After the Armistice, he was repatriated but felt he was too maimed to marry his fiancée, Dorothy. He sent her a letter breaking off their engagement. Soon afterward, there she was, marching down the hospital ward with a clergyman in tow. This photograph shows them soon after their wedding. Later, they settled in Middlebury, where Heinrichs taught American civilization at the college. (Courtesy of University of Massachusetts Amherst Library Special Collections.)

In 1942, the Vermont National Guard, along with the rest of the world, was feeling alarmed at the rate the Axis powers were running roughshod over so much of the globe. Although it appeared unthinkable, the idea of home defense was on people's minds. Here, the guard drills in the high school gym.

W. Storrs Lee first followed Gamaliel Painter's example, emigrating from Connecticut to Middlebury, where he wrote the definitive biography of Painter. Storrs Lee served in the Pacific during World War II as a naval intelligence officer. On his return, he was dean of students at the college for 10 years. He wrote 14 other books, including *Stagecoach North* and *Father Went to College*, focusing mainly on social history.

When George Commins enlisted in 1943, he became a combat medic and landed at Omaha Beach. He experienced the breaking of the Siegfried Line and the surrender of Germany. He was sent to Korea as a sergeant and encountered the Chinese at the Chosin Reservoir. On March 7, 1950, Commins earned a battlefield commission and was promoted to captain. He was also awarded the Bronze Star for bravery. On his return from combat, he met Kathleen, married her, started a family, and moved to Middlebury. This photograph was taken on their wedding day. Commins's second career was as director of custodial services for Middlebury College. He generously donated his time to the Middlebury Volunteer Ambulance Association. (Courtesy of Kevin Commins.)

Consistent with our mission to preserve history on a local level, this book was printed in South Carolina on American-made paper and manufactured entirely in the United States. Products carrying the accredited Forest Stewardship Council (FSC) label are printed on 100 percent FSC-certified paper.